MY WILD WORLD

My **WILD WORLD**

Joan Embery
with Denise Demong

DELACORTE PRESS/NEW YORK

Published by
Delacorte Press
1 Dag Hammarskjold Plaza
New York, N.Y. 10017

Manufactured in the United States of America

First printing

Designed by Laura Bernay

Library of Congress Cataloging in Publication Data

Embery, Joan.
My wild world.

Bibliography: p. 263
1. Zoo animals. 2. San Diego Zoo.
I. Demong, Denise, joint author. II. Title.
QL77.5.E47   636.08′899′0924   80-13132
ISBN 0-440-05742-6

To my mother and father,
for helping me develop the abilities
that have enabled me to have these experiences,
and for their constant support

Contents

Contents

x

Acknowledgments

My job has never been the kind that one could do alone, and some very special people have always been willing to step in and help me do it well. Among the people I want to thank are a number of San Diego Zoo personnel:

John Muth, who hired me and believed in me;

Dr. Charles Schroeder and Bill Seaton, who gave me the opportunity to be the Zoo's "goodwill ambassador," then helped me succeed at the task;

Red Thomas, Don McLennan, Robin Greenlee, Tom Schultz, and Wally Ross, all of whom worked beyond the requirements of their jobs to teach me most of what I know about handling and training animals;

JoAnn Thomas, "Boo" Shaw, Kathy Marmack, Jane Meier, and Marge Shaw, who, working diligently in the background, have been the mainstay behind many of my efforts;

xii

and Harold Darnell, who has never been too busy to stop everything and fix a halter, build a crate, or locate a prop.

I also owe a great deal to those connected with "The Tonight Show," where I got my first broad exposure on national television:

Johnny Carson, who, with his very special feeling for animals, has helped make the Zoo's public-relations efforts and my own job a success;

Craig Tennis, who gave me my first crack at the show;

Jack Grant, who always goes out of his way to accommodate me; the Zoo personnel who help me; and all the creatures we bring into the studio;

and Shirley Wood, who, following in Craig's footsteps, puts it all together.

I also thank Duane, who has given me continual emotional support and backed me up in every way.

MY WILD WORLD

1

Here's Johnny— and Joan and Carol

When Dudley Duplex, the two-headed California king snake, started crawling up Johnny Carson's sleeve, it wasn't according to the script.

But then, nothing had gone the way it was supposed to that day.

It was November 4, 1971, and I was appearing on "The Tonight Show" as the representative of the San Diego Zoo. An hour earlier, it had looked like I wasn't even going to make it to the taping.

Actually, Dudley was just a sidelight. "Tonight" was putting me on the air to show off Carol, the four-year-old Asian elephant that I had trained to paint pictures with a brush held in her trunk. Just three weeks before, the show's talent department, having heard of the Zoo's famous painting elephant, had flown me to Burbank for an interview with their talent coordinator, Craig Tennis. The show was based in New York then, but they were planning to tape some shows on the West Coast, a visit they made a few times a year. Craig wanted to meet me, see how I conducted myself in an interview, and discuss the logistics of taking an elephant on the show. Most of all, he wanted to find out whether Carol could be counted on to paint. Many trained animals become so distracted when they're outside the area in which they normally work that they won't perform. But I'd taken Carol through scores of public appearances, and she had performed successfully on a number of local San Diego and Los Angeles television shows, so I was able to assure Craig that she would indeed paint.

That settled, we had discussed additional animals that I might bring on the show and had come up with three—a hairy-nosed wombat, the two-headed snake, and a baby orangutan. Craig wanted the wombat because Johnny Carson's audience had heard again and again about this creature. There are two kinds of wombat—hairy-nosed and naked-nosed—and, at odd moments during his show, Carson was given to muttering in a W.C. Fields voice, "I think I saw a hairy-nosed wombat."

A brown furry creature, a wombat looks like some kind of rodent, but it is a marsupial, a member of that group of mammals, including the kangaroo and opossum, that raise their young in abdominal pouches. The wombat's a burrowing animal, and its pouch is inverted so that it doesn't fill up with dirt when the animal digs. It has short legs and no tail and, when fully grown, reaches a length of three feet and weighs about fifty-five pounds.

The two-headed snake seemed bound to fascinate viewers. He was about eighteen inches long, with black bands running crosswise around his body. For most of his length, he was one snake, but he did indeed have two functional heads—he was produced as the result of an incomplete twinning process. It is believed that in nature such snakes don't live very long, perhaps because the heads compete for prey, making the snake an inefficient predator. For some reason, two-headed snakes seem to be found more frequently in southern California than elsewhere, and the San Diego Zoo has had five of them—at the time we had Dudley, we had another called Nip and Tuck. The Zoo often gets letters from people saying, "I told my friend that I saw a two-headed snake in the Zoo and he didn't believe me. Can you send me a picture?" Some people just want to know if they saw what they think they saw.

Ken, the orang, was selected for the show because baby apes, which seem so much like human babies, are always a hit on television. Like all baby orangs, Ken, nicknamed Boom Orang, was wonderful to look at. He had very expressive eyes, and the hair on his head stuck straight up, almost like horns, on either side. He was kind of bow-legged, and always sat like a little Buddha, with his hands folded together and an innocent baby look on his face.

Although I'd been working for several months as the Zoo's "goodwill ambassador," making personal appearances, giving lectures, and doing local television and radio shows, I didn't realize at the outset what a coup it was, from a public-relations standpoint, to land a spot on "The Tonight Show," with a nightly viewing audience of millions. Today a thirty-second commercial spot on the show sells for about twenty to twenty-six thousand dollars.

I was just excited to be taking Carol to the show. I'd

been training her since she was a baby, and she was my buddy, my favorite animal in the whole Zoo. There was nothing I liked more than to show her off. I thought, "Carol's going to be a star; everyone's going to love her." How could anyone not love Carol the elephant?

Bill Seaton, the Zoo's PR director and my supervisor, was ecstatic about my being on the program, and when I realized that, I began to understand how important the show was to the Zoo. Then everyone around the Zoo started talking about my upcoming appearance, and my co-workers started getting excited and working extra hard to make it a good show. I started getting very nervous, realizing that I was going to be representing all of them, and that the way I came off would reflect on everyone else.

I spent the days before the show preparing, doing several hours of research on each animal so that I'd be able to speak knowledgeably, and making arrangements to transport the animals to Los Angeles. The Zoo's wombat was full grown and too vicious to be handled, but the Zoo was more than willing to accommodate any reasonable request from "The Tonight Show," so they had an elaborate viewing cage built for it. One wall was a sheet of clear Plexiglas that was covered on the inside by a sliding wood panel to keep the wombat from getting it dirty. Just before I took the wombat onstage at the NBC studio, I was to pull the wood out and reveal it behind the glass.

I started getting really jittery the day before the show, and I was up all night getting my clothes ready and studying the notes I'd made on each animal. (I've spent the night before almost every "Tonight" show that I've done since just the same way. I'm especially nervous if there's little time to prepare, but even if I have everything ready, I lie awake for hours, thinking about what I'm going to say.)

That night I worried about Carol's performance. Though I had told Craig Tennis that she would paint, I couldn't help worrying about whether I was right. NBC's Burbank studio would be bigger and busier than the studios of the shows she'd been on before. Carol was over five feet tall and weighed perhaps a ton-and-a-half, and I was only too aware that four months earlier, when I'd ridden her in a Fourth of July parade, she'd become frightened, had taken off at a run with me on her back, and had almost plunged into the side of a house. Carol had made dozens of public appearances, and that was the only time anything like that had ever happened, but it pointed up that I could never be absolutely sure of how she'd behave. It's something I've had to learn to live with as an animal handler. Many species of wild animals—or exotic animals, as we call them in the zoo world—can be conditioned to accept human contact if handled at a young enough age. But the innate aggressive and defensive behaviors that have enabled their kind to survive in the wild can never be eliminated. Most exotics are easily frightened and easily provoked, and they are never entirely reliable in their behavior. My judgment about any animal, even one that I've worked with extensively, can turn out to be mistaken.

The day of the show, Red Thomas, who worked with me as an animal handler, came along to supervise Carol, and JoAnn Thomas, head of the Zoo's nursery, came along to work with the orang. The three of us set out in the late morning in a carry-all truck with the elephant in a horse trailer behind us and the rest of the animals in the back.

We were supposed to get to the studio at three in the afternoon for a 5:30 P.M. taping, and we figured it would take about three hours to make the trip from San Diego to L.A.

Once we were on the highway, we realized that the trailer was slowing us down more than we'd anticipated, and then we began to hit heavy traffic. In California, trailers are supposed to travel in the far right-hand lane, but the far right-hand lane was hardly moving, so in desperation, Red, who was driving, pulled into the center lane. Two minutes later, we were pulled over by a highway patrolman who gave us a talking-to. Finally, we reached the outskirts of Los Angeles, only to get lost in the maze of freeways and miss our turnoff.

Our three-hour trip had stretched to more than four, and I was almost sick with anxiety by the time we pulled up behind the NBC studio to unload the animals. But there was no time to relax, because Craig Tennis came running out of the building and told me, "You're on in fifteen minutes!" If we'd arrived at three, I would have had time to change my clothes, get my hair and makeup done, settle the animals, and—most important—run Carol through her paces to get her accustomed to the studio. As it was, I just managed to dash to my dressing room and change my clothes, leaving Red and JoAnn to take care of the animals.

By the time I joined them in the dim backstage area, the show had already started—we could see Johnny Carson on the studio monitor doing his monologue. He would be announcing the wombat at any moment, but when I tried to pull the wood partition out of the wombat's cage, it jammed. When Red couldn't budge it either, I was frantic. If we couldn't get the wood out, there'd be no way for me to show the wombat, so we opened the cage door and tried to get a broom handle under the panel and push it out from the bottom. The wombat started running at us and attacking the stick so viciously that I thought one of us was going to lose his fingers. My nerves were almost shattered by the time the wood finally came free.

The cage was rolled out on a dolly, and I went on. Not only was I scared, but I felt so rushed that I could hardly think. But the cameraman photographed the wombat through the Plexiglas, and somehow I managed to talk with Johnny Carson, whom I'd never met until that moment, about the wombat's characteristics and habits.

While the wombat was being rolled off, I brought Dudley Duplex on from backstage. Johnny and I talked about the snake and I handed it to him, but Johnny lost his grip on it. That's when it started to crawl up his sleeve.

Johnny widened his eyes and rolled them back; then his expression froze and he went rigid all over. I thought of the keeper in the reptile house who had warned me, when I arranged to take Dudley to the show, that he was quite rare and I had to make sure nothing happened to him; in my mind's eye, I could see the keeper watching the show. What if, in his fright, Johnny somehow hurt the snake? Immediately, I reached over to grab Dudley, but very subtly, Johnny put his hand on mine to stop me, and I realized that he'd *let* the snake crawl up his sleeve. I sat back and watched with some astonishment—that moment probably marks the beginning of my appreciation of Carson's professional genius—and when Johnny had had his fun, he stood up and shook his arm and the snake slid out. It turned out to be an incredible spot—one that people remember to this day, and it often turns up on "Tonight Show" anniversary broadcasts.

I brought Ken Orang on next, and Johnny was clearly captivated. While I was on camera with him, Red brought Carol backstage and waited there with her. The whole area was mirrored, and every time she made a move, she could see a hundred elephants moving. When I went back to get her, I took one look and saw how nervous she was. Her ears were standing out and her eyes were so wide that the whites showed all the way around. Red handed me the bull hook with which she was handled, and I called to her and we went walking out.

My heart was pounding. How was Carol going to react to the set and the audience? And if she got really frightened, what would happen?

I can physically control most of the animals that I handle, no matter what they do. I can let them sit on my arm while I show them, but if they give me a hard time, I can grab them in a way that gives me control and allows me to talk a while longer, then exit. Certain animals, like Carol, however, are larger and stronger than I am, so there is no way I can have complete physical control over them. I have to be able to count on other things: in Carol's case, that she was well trained and trusted me. An animal that is excited can feel comforted by a handler's confidence.

Carol did settle right down, and, brush in trunk, she began painting with all her usual enthusiasm. She had a tendency to swing her trunk as she turned to look at people standing next to her, and she painted the floor and Johnny and made a bit of a mess before she got through. But I was right. Everybody loved her. How could anyone not love Carol the elephant?

2

Zoo Story

I had fallen in love with Carol the first time I'd ever set eyes on her, three and a half years before. She was about a year old then and about three feet tall—a big, almost-pink-skinned, awkward, comical baby. It was my first day of work as an attendant in the San Diego Zoo's Children's Zoo, and one of my jobs was to "baby-sit" for her.

When I'd visited the Zoo as a child, I'd always dreamed of working with the baby elephants, and now, hard as it was to believe, I was standing inside their enclosure, tending them.

All my life, I had wanted more than anything to work with animals for a living. People often ask, "When did you begin getting interested in animals?" "When did you decide you wanted to have a career involving animals?" But I don't remember any turning point. If your family is interested in animals, I'm sure you're more likely to become an "animal person," and I grew up in a family that loves animals. My uncle is a vet and my mother worked for many years as a vet's assistant. We—my parents, my two sisters and I—always lavished affection on the animals we had.

When I was a kid, I never could get enough pets. I kept whatever animals I could convince my parents to take on. We had all the typical pet shop animals—dogs, rabbits, ducks, chickens, and guinea pigs—and abandoned wild creatures, like possums, snakes, and squirrels.

My special love was horses, and when I was little, I spent every Christmas Eve looking out the window, expecting to see a pony. I don't think I ever really wanted anything else. In the back of my mind, I knew it wasn't possible—we lived in the city of San Diego, and we couldn't afford a horse anyway. But I always hoped that I just might be surprised and have my wish come true. When I was in junior high school, I finally started taking riding lessons, and I started showing horses as soon as I got my first job and could afford to pay the cost.

I decided when I was very young that I wanted to become a veterinarian, partly because it was the only animal-related career with which I was familiar. As children, my twin sister, Linda, and I used to spend every summer with our uncle and his family in Santa Cruz, and I was fascinated by my visits to his veterinary hospital. I was also interested in the stories my mother told when she came home from work, but she worked with small animals, like cats and dogs, and I was more interested in large animals. Uncle Gene worked with both. He had an office where people brought pets and small animals, and he went out on calls to treat sheep, cattle, and horses.

The thrill of each summer visit was being able to go through the clinic and see all the animals there. Linda wasn't as interested as I was, and my uncle's kids, who'd grown up with it, never thought twice about his profession. To them, it meant hard work—they had to clean kennels and do other chores. But I couldn't understand how they could take it all for granted. I thought it was exciting to see the animals all bandaged after surgery. I always had to find out the history of each one and what it was doing there.

Sometimes I watched my uncle do surgery, and I don't remember ever feeling squeamish about it. Because of my mom's work, our conversations at home every night at the dinner table had often been about veterinary emergencies, and we'd gotten so that we'd sit there eating dinner, talking about blood and guts and thinking absolutely nothing of it. That helped to prepare me for the occasions when animals became sick when I later worked at the Zoo. Some people who work at the Zoo have been so removed from hospitals and treatments and suffering that it's tough for them to handle it when an animal is sick or injured. I'm accustomed to it, though when a person gets hurt, I don't handle it very well. To tell the truth, I even passed out once when I had blood taken from my arm for a blood test.

I used to love to go out with my uncle when he went on calls in his truck, which was equipped with instruments for handling veterinary emergencies. I remember one emergency call from a summer camp where the owners had built a horse stall in an apple orchard. Their horse had eaten pounds and pounds of green apples and had developed colic. Horses can't vomit, and when they get colic, they develop a terrible cramp in the stomach. When we arrived at the camp, the horse, which was still in the corral where he'd gotten sick, was sweating all over and biting his sides. Soon he lay down and began to thrash around. It was frightening, because colic can kill horses. Sometimes, by thrashing, a horse actually twists its intestine, causing a fatal blockage, and sometimes it dies from shock induced by the pain.

My uncle quickly set to work. While the owner held the horse's head and I handed my uncle equipment, he ran a tube through the horse's nostril, all the way down into its stomach, and pumped in medication. Then he gave the horse a shot to relax its muscles. The horse was still very sick when we left, but when we checked on him the next day, he'd come out of it okay. I was impressed by my uncle's work, but I was also a bit intimidated. I wondered if I could ever learn to handle such big animals.

Nobody in my family ever discouraged me from trying to be a veterinarian. My parents did try to get me to think about teaching, because there was greater opportunity in that field, and I didn't get the kind of grades that would assure my acceptance by a veterinary school. But certainly no one ever suggested that I couldn't be a veterinarian because I was a girl; in fact, my uncle did all he could to encourage me.

After I finished high school, I enrolled at San Diego State University as a pre-vet major. About the same time, I started trying to get a job working with animals, because I was told that practical experience was an important consideration for admission to veterinary school.

I thought it would be terrific to work with exotic animals, so I applied for jobs at the only two places in San Diego where it was possible to work with them—at the Zoo, and at Sea World, the marine aquarium. At each, only one job that involved direct contact with animals was open to women. At the Zoo, I applied to be an attendant in the Children's Zoo, and at Sea World, I applied to be one of the "sea maids" who swam underwater with the dolphins. My chances of getting either job were pretty slim.

I also applied to several San Diego veterinary clinics. I would have been happy to get any job that involved working with animals, but I wanted the job at the Zoo most of all.

I'd been visiting the Zoo since I was a child. My earliest memory of it is of falling into the duck pond, and on another occasion, I wandered away from my family and got lost, and someone delivered me to the security office and got me an ice cream cone. But my fondest memories are of the elephants, which I always loved best of all the animals.

Even after I'd started high school, the Zoo was my favorite place to go on a date—no wonder my classmates thought I was obsessed with animals! But there were more things to see there than I could ever hope to have time to see; I could have gone there every day.

The Zoo's a place of truly spectacular beauty. As soon as you've stepped through the gate, it's almost impossible to believe that you're in the city of San Diego. You're in a tropical jungle containing animals from all over the world in enclosures spread over mesas and canyons. There are palm trees and abundant foliage everywhere, and animal smells mingle with the sweet scent of tropical blossoms, for this is not only an outstanding zoo, but a fabulous botanical garden. There are always thousands of visitors. Every few minutes, tour buses run by driver-guides roll through. For people on foot, there are "moving sidewalks"—escalatorlike ramps—to carry them up the steeper hills. The Skyfari aerial tram, six stories up, runs from one end of the Zoo to the other, offering passengers a good overview not only of the Zoo, but—on a clear day—of much of the city as well.

The Zoo, San Diego's leading tourist attraction, is located in Balboa Park, a city park that also contains the Old Globe Theater, the Natural History Museum, the Museum of Man, the Space Theater, and the Aerospace Museum. Established in 1916, it has long been considered one of the finest zoos in the world.

Zoos can be compared in various terms—by their geographic size, by the number of animals they have, by the number and kind of different species they have, by the design of their enclosures and graphic displays, by their breeding records, and by their research and education activities. Some zoos have few animals but display them beautifully—they do well with what they have. The San Diego Zoo's reputation is outstanding because the Zoo ranks very high in all categories.

The Zoo is relatively small in geographic size—only 128 acres. But the Wild Animal Park, a breeding preserve established as an adjunct to the Zoo in 1972, is much larger than most zoos in this country. Located some thirty miles north of the Zoo but still within San Diego city limits, it contains 1,800 acres, 600 of which have been developed so far.

The Zoo is world famous for its many kinds of animals. There are about 3,000 animals—some 750 species—at the Zoo, and some 3,250 animals—260 species—at the Wild Animal Park. They include some of the rarest animals on earth. Just as everyone knows the Washington, D.C., Zoo for its pandas, everyone knows the San Diego Zoo for its koalas—it's the only zoo outside of Australia that has them. It's the only zoo in this country that has Komodo "dragons," which, at ten feet in length, are the largest lizards in existence. Presently, the San Diego Zoo is also the only zoo that has both male and female kiwis—nocturnal, flightless birds from New Zealand—though the National Zoo in Washington, D.C., and the Brookfield Zoo in Chicago both have males. Many of the animals in the San Diego Zoo are seen in few zoos anywhere in the world. To go to one zoo and see okapis—rare, short-necked members of the giraffe family; pygmy chimpanzees; kiwis; koalas; and Komodo dragons—as one can in San Diego—is an extraordinary experience.

The Zoo's uniquely designed enclosures and displays are among its biggest attractions. Moats, which take the place of fences in most of the displays, give the Zoo an open look and are more appealing than cages. The warm, dry San Diego climate—southern California sunshine blesses the Zoo about 330 days of every year—makes it possible to display animals outside the year round. The money that zoos in other parts of the country have to spend on buildings can be spent on beautiful plant-filled outdoor displays that give the Zoo the feeling of a natural environment.

The displays are augmented with information on how each animal fits into the ecological system. Enclosures depict natural habitats, and outside most of them are illustrated signs showing each species's outstanding physical characteristics, geographic range, and relationship to other species. A few years ago, one only found such information in dioramas at a natural history museum, but modern zoos use displays and graphics as educational tools. Though visitors generally go to zoos to be entertained, most zoo professionals hope they'll learn something while they're there. Sophisticated graphic designs communicate even to visitors who don't speak English.

The warm climate not only makes it possible to have beautiful open enclosures, but enables the Zoo to maintain its fantastic botanical collection. Some 3,000 species of plants, including bamboo, orchids, palms, bananas, fig trees, cacti, aloes, and ferns, grow on the Zoo grounds. Wherever feasible, plants and animals from the same geographic location are displayed together. The botanical collection is worth at least as much as—and some people say it's worth more than—the animal collection. But there is such abundance that many of the botanical exhibits are fed to the animals.

Indeed, the mild climate and the presence of eucalyptus are what have made it possible for the Zoo to maintain koalas successfully. Koalas require a diet of several kinds of eucalyptus—there are 600 in all—and the Zoo has some 35 varieties, of which 16 are fed to the koalas.

Since the turn of the century, more than forty animal species have been eliminated from the face of the earth. While most people seem to think that hunting is to blame for the eradication of wild animal populations, the major cause is the destruction of natural habitats as man competes with animal for space and food. Today, more than a thousand species of birds, mammals, and reptiles are "endangered"—unlikely to survive if the factors causing their declining numbers continue to operate—and at the present rate, twenty-five more species can be expected to become extinct in the next ten years.

The plight of animals in the wild has wrought a major change in the function of zoos. Historically, a zoo existed simply to exhibit live exotic animals for the entertainment and education of people who couldn't travel around the world to see them in their natural environments. Today, many zoos put a major emphasis on successful captive reproduction of their animals and are working to become self-sufficient, to eliminate the need to import animals from the wild. Consequently, zoos have begun to play a crucial role in the conservation of exotic animals. Already there are numerous species that are extinct in the wild and are perpetuated only in captive environments.

The San Diego Zoo is dedicated to the conservation of exotic animals in the wild wherever possible and participates in worldwide conservation programs. But the Zoo is also dedicated to fulfilling its modern role as a preserve for endangered species. The Wild Animal Park, where animals are maintained in large ranges under conditions kept as close to nature as possible, is the embodiment of this dedication. Even before the establishment of the Wild Animal Park, the Zoo was known for its outstanding breeding programs, but at the Park, such animals as cheetahs and rhinoceroses, which had never bred at the Zoo, have reproduced successfully.

The Zoo and Park have excellent research departments, which, through their work in zoo medicine, animal behavior, nutrition, and disease control, have developed procedures that enable exotic animals to live longer and reproduce more successfully in captivity. None of this research involves killing or performing otherwise unnecessary surgery on animals. Sometimes, if an animal is undergoing a needed surgical procedure and is anesthetized, the veterinarians take advantage of the situation and do a biopsy or draw blood for research purposes, and additional research materials are gathered during the post-mortem examinations performed on every animal that dies at the Zoo or Park. A great deal of our research, however, is behavioral. Because of its large collection and excellent facilities, the Zoo gets cooperation in its research programs from universities, research clinics, and hospitals.

At its founding, the Zoo was dedicated to San Diego's children, and that commitment is reflected today in the activities of the education department, which offers tours, lectures, and classes to over 250,000 people a year. Annual conducted tours for all second-grade students in San Diego City and County are a Zoo tradition.

You had to be eighteen to work with animals at the Zoo, and I applied when I was seventeen and a half. Then I started calling and going there, only to be frustrated by the number of job applications on file and the fact that I got no reassurance at all from any of the people in the personnel office. (Working with animals, naturally, is a fantasy job for animal lovers. Today, ten thousand people have active job applications on file at the San Diego Zoo and Wild Animal Park, where there are only 800 people on the entire staff. Sea World also has 10,000 applications on file.) I'd get all dressed up and go in to see the Zoo personnel people; I'd take whatever classes I thought would be helpful, but I didn't seem to be getting anywhere.

At the end of my freshman year in college—after nearly a year of this—I was ready to give up. I made a pact with myself. I would call the Zoo just one more time. If they didn't hire me, it wasn't meant to be—I'd leave them alone and concentrate my efforts elsewhere. I made the call and listened with disappointment as the woman in the personnel department told me once again that there were no positions open, that there probably wouldn't be any in the near future, and that they'd let me know if anything came up. It seemed so much like a rote negative reply that was handed out to anyone calling for a job that I figured there was no chance I'd ever be hired.

But the next day, the Zoo called. There was an opening for a Children's Zoo attendant. They wanted to know if I was still available and whether I could come in for an interview with the manager of the Children's Zoo immediately.

Nervous and excited, I got all dressed up in a blue outfit and white high-heeled shoes and drove to the Zoo. After the man in charge of interviewing personnel talked with me, he took me to meet John Muth, the Children's Zoo manager, who was waiting in his second-story office, which was enclosed by big windows offering a bird's-eye view of the Children's Zoo and everyone who worked there. He was a big man, tan, with a crew cut, very pleasant but very stern—he made me feel that if I didn't toe the line, I'd be fired in no time. In fact, he said as much. "We've gotten along without you and we can continue to get along without you," he told me. "We haven't had any trouble, and if we have trouble after you're here, we'll get rid of you."

He explained that taking the job would mean working weekends and being on call—I wouldn't have regular hours but would be called in when someone else was sick or wanted the day off. But by then, I was ready to do anything. When he told me I'd start work the next day, I was ecstatic.

3

Growing Up with the Animals

My first day with all the animals was like seventh heaven. All the times I'd visited the Children's Zoo in the past, I'd been on the outside looking in, and suddenly I was being taken inside. I felt like an honored guest, finally able to touch everything and see what goes on beyond the public view.

The Children's Zoo, a one-and-one-third-acre area within the main zoo, is designed especially for kids and holds young animals that they can view at close range. There have been many changes made in the Children's Zoo since the time I worked there, but now, as then, it's the Zoo's number-one attraction.

The animals there, chosen to appeal to children, include domestic animals as well as young exotics that have been raised in nurseries within the Children's Zoo because they were orphaned, abandoned, or sickly babies. The Children's Zoo is entertaining, but it also serves an essential function. The exotics there are in a transitional stage; though they've outgrown the nursery, they aren't yet able to hold their own among adult animals. The petting areas and close-contact areas in the Children's Zoo are their home from about the time they're weaned until they've matured enough to be moved to the main zoo.

When I worked in the Children's Zoo, it housed guinea pigs, snakes, squirrels, goats, sheep, and small birds. The exotics included llamas and tapir from the hoofstock nursery; baby lions, cheetahs, apes, and monkeys from the main nursery; and baby elephants. (Because bull elephants are very difficult to control, the Zoo keeps only females, which are acquired while they are still young for the Children's Zoo and moved to the main zoo as display animals when they grow up. Since the spacious Wild Animal Park was established in 1972, a young bull Asian elephant and a bull African elephant have been acquired, and an elephant breeding program has been undertaken.)

The doors, displays, drinking fountains, and toilets in the Children's Zoo were all sized to accommodate children. The windows of the nocturnal rodent house were two-and-one-half feet off the ground, instead of four, and the moats surrounding the other displays were just high enough to contain the animals, but low enough so children could see over them.

Many of the animals could be petted. In the paddock area, children mingled with goats and sheep and occasionally young exotics like camels and gazelles. There was a large Galápagos tortoise they could ride on. There was a chicken brooder, where they could watch baby chicks pecking their way out of their shells, and there was a whole batch of chicks they could pick up and pet. The cats could be petted through a fence made of a close-mesh wire just big enough for a child to get a finger through to stroke a fuzzy ear, and the kids could also get very close to the apes, though they were not allowed to touch them.

The areas of the Children's Zoo where they had the closest contact with the animals were the areas that young visitors enjoyed most. Though there were seals and cheetahs and a koala on display, the kids would just glance at them as they ran on in to the paddock or chick-hatching display. The glass-walled nursery, where newborn creatures could be seen getting careful attention from substitute human mothers, was also a favorite spot.

Changes made in the Children's Zoo since the time I worked there reflect increased liability consciousness and new attitudes about the proper way to handle animals. There's still a chicken brooder, but the kids are no longer allowed to pick up the chicks, and there's no longer a tortoise for them to ride because Galápagos tortoises are now protected as an endangered species. The displays of young apes and cats have been eliminated entirely; today animals of both families are moved directly to the main zoo as soon as they're old enough to leave the nursery. In the case of the apes, it's desirable to minimize their contact with people, because, while many animals take on instinctive behavior, apes learn their behavior. If they're raised by humans, they may not mix well when they're put with other apes. Close contact with visitors was also eliminated because apes are susceptible to many diseases transmitted among humans; in fact, the apes in the Zoo routinely receive vaccinations against diseases like measles and polio.

* * *

When I was in the Children's Zoo, there was an attendant on duty to answer questions and supervise the contact between animals and people at each enclosure where visitors and animals were in close proximity. Otherwise, visitors might harass the animals, and the animals, because of their instinctive defensive behavior, might frighten the people. Attendants also helped feed, care for, and clean up after the animals. There were eight of us on duty every day; most were college-age girls like me.

During my first three days of work, I followed one of the senior girls around in order to learn the ropes. I wasn't exactly frightened, but I didn't know what the animals were going to do, and I'd never been so close to an elephant in my life.

Each attendant spent half an hour twice a day at each supervised area. My day began with a half hour spent with the baby elephants, then a half hour sitting inside a covered pen containing the two young cheetahs. From there I'd move into the paddock, then to an area where there were young sea lions or harbor seals, then to the ape enclosure, over to the spider monkeys, and finally, to the chick-hatching display. After a lunch break, I'd start again with the elephants, so in the course of a day, I'd spend a total of an hour at each point.

Attendants also did certain chores each morning and evening. The girls with the most seniority got to choose their jobs, and usually they chose to feed and bathe the apes, take the cats to their enclosure, or feed the elephants and prepare their area. Those of us with the least seniority got stuck cleaning the chicken brooder and scrubbing the kitchen floors. We all wore white uniforms—pants and shirt with a Children's Zoo emblem—and it was just impossible to keep them clean. I, especially, became known for ending up covered with dirt by the end of the day.

During my training, I was assigned to work in the hoof-stock nursery. I was cutting up fruits and vegetables for the young animals when the girl who was training me exclaimed, "What are you doing?" She pulled the food dishes I'd filled out of the pens and just shook her head, because the amount of food I'd given the animals actually exceeded their body weight. But I wanted to make sure all the animals had plenty to eat.

Working in the Children's Zoo is the dream job of many of San Diego's college girls, but quite a few who start working there don't stay with it. Some think they're going to get to play with animals all day, but they soon find out that a big part of the job is cleaning up after the animals and supervising people. It can be hard, dirty work. In the summer, it means spending most of the day working in the hot sun. If there's a harsh winter, it's long hours out in the cold and rain.

In the beginning, the only time I got to work was when someone else was sick. I used to sit by the phone every morning hoping it would ring. Until the school year ended, I skipped class to work if necessary.

I really loved that job. If I hadn't felt that way, I couldn't have stuck it out. I couldn't go away on weekends, and I couldn't do things with my friends if they were leaving in the morning. I couldn't plan ahead. I might work three days one week and then not work at all for the next two weeks. There were so many part-time girls at work that it took a while to develop enough seniority to have regular hours.

Before I got to know him, John Muth scared me because

he was so brusque, but I soon realized that though he was stern on the outside, he was very warm, almost sentimental, on the inside. Perhaps he tried to cover it. He always looked a bit gruff until he smiled, and then he didn't look gruff at all.

Still, people always mentioned that he was a former marine corps officer, and he did run the Children's Zoo a bit like the military. Most Zoo employees can be identified by their enormous bunches of keys—every enclosure is locked, and different types of keys are used in different departments. You can't get anywhere without keys, and my biggest problem when I first started was that I was always losing mine. Finally John made me drag around a huge boat chain, nearly as heavy as I was, to impress upon me the importance of not losing my keys. I felt like Marley's ghost in Dickens's *A Christmas Carol*. But to this day, even though I carry my keys on a huge brass ring, I often don't know where they are. Whenever keys are found, the security guards call me first to see if they're mine.

For a while, I was caught up in the novelty of the Children's Zoo, and then I started trying to learn everything I could about working with animals. My only experience when I started was caring for my own pets, raising the small wild creatures that I'd brought home as a kid, and showing other people's horses for them. I'd never been around exotic animals at all.

I had plenty to learn. If you read and study, you can learn animal statistics, and where various animals come from, and animal biology. But the only way to become a good animal handler is to handle a lot of animals.

The handling the attendants had to do was very elementary. We had to move the animals from one spot to another to feed and clean up after them, but we weren't expected to control them the way I have to today in order to take animals on television. Still, I learned a lot just by being around so many kinds of animals.

No matter how well trained an exotic animal is, it never loses the defensive traits that have been bred into its species for thousands of years as it evolved and adapted to its environment. (Domestic animals, by contrast, have been selectively bred over and over to eliminate aggressive tendencies, so that people can handle them and raise them for food, as work animals, and for companionship. Dogs are believed to have been domesticated as early as 1,000 to 12,000 years ago, and sheep and goats have been domesticated nearly as long. The domestication of cattle, pigs, donkeys, and horses goes back to at least 3000 B.C.)

Most exotics show aggression out of fear. They can be frightened by an individual, a sound, or any number of things. Scientists have described so-called "flight distances"—specific distances, different for different species, which animals have to place between themselves and things that threaten them in order to feel safe. A handler has to determine how close somebody can get by watching the reactions of each animal.

When frightened, most exotic animals try to get away from whatever it is that frightens them, rather than to attack. They attack when they feel trapped, when the only way they can get away is to attack whatever is restraining them. The problem an animal handler faces when working closely with exotics is that they can't be let go, because they're dangerous when they're frightened. If an animal gets excited, you have to handle it the best way you can and get it under control—by putting it back in its cage or restraining it or eliminating whatever is frightening it.

But if you're hanging on to a frightened animal, it may become aggressive toward you, because you're keeping it from fleeing.

The first thing many people ask about my work is whether I'm afraid. You can't be a good animal handler if you're really frightened, because your fear inhibits your ability; when you're scared, you're more likely to do something that will scare an animal or let go of an animal that you shouldn't let go of. You do have to have respect for an animal's destructive capabilities, and that's hard to teach many people. But someone who has no respect for an animal is someone who's going to get hurt.

One reason exotic animals are dangerous is that they seem to be—but aren't really—reliable in their behavior. If keepers or handlers are lulled into a sense of security, they're unprepared when an animal behaves erratically.

Working in the Children's Zoo was an ideal learning situation, because most of the animals were young and not as dangerous as they would be as adults, and I had a chance to grow up with them. As they matured, I watched them take on more typical wild animal behavior and saw that lions behave in certain ways and elephants in other ways—each species has particular tendencies. The animals I was allowed to handle were moved out of the Children's Zoo before they became threatening, so I developed confidence in working with them. There's a continual turnover of animals in the Children's Zoo, and in a couple of years I worked with a tremendous variety.

4

My Love Affair with Elephants

There were actually two baby elephants in the Children's Zoo, but it was Carol that won my heart. The other was Sumithi, a Ceylonese elephant, very cute, with long orange bangs all the way down to her eyes. She was lovable and sweet, but very timid and standoffish, and nervous about being told to do anything. She used to sit back in the corner and watch while Carol came running up to me.

Carol was very inquisitive. The first time I went into the elephant enclosure, she walked right up to me and began to sniff me all over, even thrusting the moist tip of her trunk into my face, not grabbing me, but almost petting me. Baby elephants' trunks hang kind of limp—they have to learn to use them—and Carol wrapped hers around me with baby clumsiness. I thought she was the most fascinating creature in the whole Zoo.

29

One reason I'd always loved elephants is that they're tremendously intelligent and, I think as a direct consequence of that intelligence, they have distinct individual personalities. True to their reputation, they have good memories. They're very social animals, and most of them seem to like to be with and please people.

Visitors could reach across a low moat to pet the baby elephants, so there was an attendant in their enclosure at all times. We were supposed to keep the elephants off the sides of the moat so that they wouldn't fall down inside of it, and keep them from grabbing purses and things from visitors. I was given a rounded wooden cane called an ankus or bull hook, and taught how to use it to control them.

Elephants are trained to move away from various sensitive points when pressure is applied with the ankus. It's somewhat similar to the way horses are trained, to move away from pressure applied by a rider's legs. The trainer has to communicate, to get the elephant to understand what it's supposed to do. If I tapped Carol at the bottom of her foot, I could get her to lift it—away from the pressure. Then I'd reward her with food or praise, to let her know that was just what I wanted her to do.

When confronted with anything threatening, an elephant is likely to run away or fight, so it has to be trained to accept the cues given with the hook. Introduction to the bull hook is also an elephant's first experience of being controlled, and some resist, while others accept it easily. It's important to start training early, when the elephant is still small enough to be restrained.

The elephants had to be disciplined. If Carol grabbed me with her trunk, I'd swat her. Her trunk was sensitive, so she didn't like that. But she grabbed me again and again before she began to understand that every time she did, I'd smack the tip of her trunk. Or that every time she kicked me, I'd slap her foot with a stick. You can't allow an elephant to do such things. It starts with a cute little grab, and the next thing you know she's getting very aggressive, and when she gets bigger, she starts pulling you off your feet and can throw you on the ground. Then you can't handle her at all, and neither can anyone else.

When exotic animals are maintained in captivity, those that will be handled as adults have to be subjected to training and discipline. Only a small percentage of the adult animals in the Zoo are ever handled, but the elephants have to be continuously handled and disciplined for practical reasons. They must be manageable enough for keepers to trim their toenails (in captivity elephants rarely walk enough to wear away their nails as they do in the wild) and oil their skin to keep it from drying out. (In nature, elephants cover themselves with mud for the same reason, and while there are pools and mud holes for the elephants at the Zoo and Park, additional protection is sometimes necessary.) Even more important, because the elephants are handled regularly, keepers and vets can go to the assistance of a sick or injured elephant without having to anesthetize it.

The longer you wait to begin training an elephant, the tougher it is to establish discipline. The same is true of domestic animals such as dogs and horses, though they don't grow to as dangerous a size as elephants. A "rogue" or bad elephant is usually knocked around from one zoo to another until somebody finally decides that it can't be safely managed, and then it's destroyed because it's dangerous. All the elephants that passed through the Children's Zoo were taught to walk forward and back up on command, to stay in one position, to pick up a foot so that a leg chain could be put on or taken off for night security, and to "lead"—meaning to follow a trainer closely, neither running ahead nor lagging behind.

There are some people who are opposed to animal training, who say that anything that molds an animal is wrong because it's unnatural, but I disagree. In the wild, animals are very much molded, by their environment and by other animals. They have distinct social patterns, and they sometimes get rougher with one another in establishing their social order than I would ever get in training.

In the wild, when baby elephants walk up to a feeding area, the other elephants accommodate them and even help them find food. But as they get older, the other elephants become less accommodating. If a young cow interferes with another's eating, the older elephant will kick or slap her away. Eventually the young bulls are actually run out of the herd and become solitary.

Sometimes I think that the Zoo animals look to establish their position, to find out where they fit in the scheme of things. Because of the social hierarchy maintained by animals in the wild, one has to function in a dominant role to work with most animals. Depending on the circumstances, almost any exotic animal past babyhood can be dangerous. An ape at 40 pounds, an elephant weighing 500 pounds or more, a cat three to four months old or older— once an animal becomes strong enough to strike back at you or take off, your physical control is limited. You have to reach a point where you have mental control—that's what discipline is all about.

Some people advocate "affection training" or "love training," but it has a limited effect. It depends on a somewhat

anthropomorphic point of view—the basic principle behind it is that if you love an animal, it will love you back;
if you show an animal that you will never hurt it or harm
it, it will never hurt or harm you. While it's true that con-
veying affection and calmness to an excited animal will
help calm it down, it's also true that if it gets frightened,
it'll still turn around and bite you, regardless of how much
love and affection you've shown it. You might be able to
go into an enclosure with an animal that's known nothing
but kindness, but you'll have little control over it. Affection training is not training in the sense that I use the
word—to mean disciplined behavior.

Some of the girls in the Children's Zoo were frightened
by the elephants or just weren't very interested in them.
A lot of them fell in love with the baby cheetahs, so I
started trading off my time with the cheetahs for time with
the elephants. I traded with anybody who was willing;
sometimes I'd manage three hours a day with Carol and
Sumithi.

The remarkable subtleties of elephant intelligence and
personality were revealed to me every day. Even their
special physical attributes were fascinating. I was aston-
ished to discover that the bottoms of their feet were soft,
like pads, not hard, and I loved watching Carol and
Sumithi learn to use their trunks as the versatile tools they
are. Carol didn't like the peafowl that wander freely
through the Zoo, and if they came too close to her, she'd
screech at them and even throw dirt and rocks to drive
them away.

One of her favorite things was the swimming pool inside
the enclosure. She'd get right in it and play, and I soon

learned that she liked to get under the hose and open her mouth and have me spray water into it. She'd let out a high-pitched squeal and run in and out of the pool like a little kid, splashing water all over the place.

One of my responsibilities was to feed the elephants. When Carol got her bucket of fruits and vegetables, she would pull out all the sweet potatoes and throw them on the ground, smashing them with her feet. She always seemed very insulted about it. But Sumithi obviously loved sweet potatoes; she gobbled them right down. And the elephants never just put hay in their mouths. They picked it up, folded it neatly into a little pile, and then ate it.

In those days—though no longer—Zoo visitors were allowed to feed certain animals, including the elephants. Carol would eat until she was kind of full and then she'd get choosy—she'd pick up what people gave her and look it over, and if it was something better than usual, she'd eat it, and if it was something she didn't have a real interest in, she'd toss it in the moat.

Unfortunately, a lot of people would tease. They'd only pretend they had food, or they'd proffer food, then pull it away. Carol would slap them right in the face with her trunk, as if to say, "I'll show you what happens when you tease me!" She knew what it was to be disciplined for misbehaving. She was justified—the people weren't being nice—but I had to discipline her if she did that, because we didn't want her to get in the habit of slapping people. Even a baby elephant can knock somebody flat on his back. Carol had a real sense of justice, and she'd actually pout if I disciplined her and she thought it was undeserved. She'd let her trunk hang real limp and just sit with her eyes half closed and do nothing, as if to say, "Aw shucks, I was only kidding, don't hit me."

My Love Affair with Elephants

The elephants were so smart, they even knew how to play dumb. They obviously recognized many of the Zoo sounds—I would always see them perk up when they heard the wheels of the cart that brought their food to them—but often when I was telling them to do something, they'd pretend they didn't hear me, as if they thought that if they ignored me I might just go away. When a new attendant came into the Children's Zoo, I could almost see them plotting, "Okay, we've got a new baby-sitter today. Let's see if she's a disciplinarian or if she's afraid of us or if she likes to play." They knew which girls in the Children's Zoo they could push around, and they had their favorites and those they didn't like. They had everybody completely figured out.

Carol always wanted to be involved, to be on top of everything I did. I'd sit down in the enclosure and she'd come and literally sit on my lap, even though she weighed four or five hundred pounds. As she got even bigger, of course, I had to break her of that habit, but she just liked to be close to people. She'd go get something and bring it over to me, or she'd get herself in trouble with things she wasn't supposed to be doing, crawling on the side of the moat or grabbing people's purses. Sometimes she'd do something she knew she wasn't supposed to do, and then stand there and look at me to see what I was going to do about it. I realized how smart she was and saw that she just had to be busy all the time and to involve me in whatever she was doing. So I started training her.

I did it just to entertain myself, relying on my background with horses and dogs. Such training techniques as reward and discipline are very similar for all animals. In the beginning, Carol was small enough to be handled much like a pet. I would tell her to sit and push her hind

end down, and when she sat, I'd give her a carrot or an apple and tell her how good she was. With repetition, sitting in response to my cue became what behaviorists call a "conditioned response."

Communication is at the heart of training. You can't teach an animal to do anything if it doesn't understand what you expect it to do. You have to put yourself in the animal's situation—if you were an elephant, how could you be made to understand what behavior is wanted? You have to be very distinct about what you're asking an animal to do, and you have to follow through, exaggerating your praise when it does what you want.

To teach Carol to pick up an object, I'd put it on the ground, and every time she grasped it, I would tell her what a good girl she was and give her some food, or pat her and encourage her. If an elephant won't pick things up that way, you wrap its trunk around whatever it is you want it to grasp, hold the trunk that way and feed the animal, doing it over and over until the elephant will hold it itself. Carol was kind of aggressive and wanted to be into everything, so she picked things up without reluctance, while a less inquisitive elephant might have required more prodding.

An animal has to be made comfortable before any communication is possible. You can't teach an animal anything when it's frightened by its surroundings or if it feels that you're a threat. You don't have the animal's attention. A good trainer has to sense what makes an animal comfortable and realize when it's at ease and when it's not.

Training requires discipline and reward in the proper combination. Discipline can take the form of withholding the animal's reward, or it can be a matter of keeping after the animal until it does what you want correctly. When I was training Carol, I'd keep asking her to sit, making her do it again and again until she got it right, and then I'd give her food.

If you always discipline an animal, but never reward it, it doesn't know when it's right, and it has no reason to want to work. If you get too rough, an animal won't respond, because it's too frightened to learn anything. All it wants to do is get away from you, or come after you, if it feels so threatened that it has to be aggressive.

For Carol, training provided stimulation and a challenge. She was always eager to work. Elephants vocalize, or talk, and from the way Carol talked and flapped her ears, you could tell how much she loved training. I think she looked upon it as a game. She usually tried hard to do what I wanted and to do it right.

The first day I taught her a particular command, I could easily spend three or four hours, even the whole day, getting her to understand what I wanted her to do. The second day I might spend an hour, and the third day it might take half an hour. Once communication was established, it was just a matter of molding the pattern as precisely as I wanted and associating a voice command or other cue with whatever it was I was asking her to do.

Carol learned to do most things very readily. I started with simple commands and progressed from there. The hardest part of training is always getting the first couple of ideas across. Once Carol understood that I was asking something of her, and that when she did the right thing she'd be rewarded, she'd try a number of different things and run through everything she'd already learned, trying to figure out what I was looking for.

I progressed by putting together all the bits and pieces that everybody around the Children's Zoo knew about

38

training elephants. It's hard to remember where I picked things up; I was like a big sponge. Within a year, Carol was pretty well obedience-trained. She would lift up her trunk or foot, sit, stay and come, pick up and carry things, and follow other basic commands.

In time, Carol got to the age, as all animals in the Children's Zoo do, when she was going to have to move on. She was getting big—baby elephants gain an average of two pounds a day or 60 pounds a month—and she was starting to misbehave and push people around. When people would tease or play with her, she'd bully them, and she was beginning to learn that she could intimidate some of the other girls, who were afraid to discipline her. One day she knocked the daughter of one of the Zoo's trustees into the swimming pool—talk about choosing the wrong attendant to pick on. A man jumped in to help the girl and ended up getting a bravery award from the phone company, which I thought was a little excessive—though Carol was getting aggressive, she was still just a young elephant. Still, it was decided that Carol had to be moved out. I was terrified. If Carol left the Children's Zoo, that would mean the end of my contact with her, and she and I had become almost inseparable!

I knew that ultimately she would have to leave. But I fought and fought, did everything but lose my job trying to explain to the Children's Zoo officials that it wasn't Carol's fault. Part of the problem was that she had people buffaloed, and they were allowing her to take advantage. When the management relented and agreed to keep Carol in the Children's Zoo a while longer, I heaved a sigh of relief. What I didn't know was that I would be the first to leave the Children's Zoo to go to the main zoo.

5

*Animal
Ambassador*

In the fall of 1968, the Zoo's public relations department announced the search for an attractive young woman to work as the Zoo's representative, making public appearances, talking about the Zoo, and handling animals. This "goodwill ambassador" would pose for publicity photographs with animals, give short talks before local organizations, take VIPs on Zoo tours, and travel for the Zoo in a public-relations capacity.

The idea was borrowed from Disneyland, where each year a different girl was chosen to go on promotional tours. The Zoo frequently provided animals for public functions, and there were bound to be more special events than ever during 1969, the bicentennial of the city of San Diego. There was extra excitement at the Zoo, too, where plans were moving ahead for establishment of the Wild Animal Park.

Promotional appearances are vital to the Zoo's very survival, because the Zoo is self-supporting. Most zoos are supported by their cities as a part of the park system and are operated by city governments, frequently by the park commission. The San Diego Zoo—the land, the animals and all the structures and physical entities within—belongs to the city of San Diego, but the Zoo is operated by a private zoological society as a nonprofit organization, separate from the city government.

The San Diego Zoological Society has a Board of Trustees that determines policy, and a director who carries out that policy. The Board has twelve members, mostly prominent San Diego businesspeople who serve without pay. Various committees made up of Zoo staff members and volunteer consultants decide how funds should be spent, and the director conveys their opinions to the Board for approval.

Most of us who work there consider the Zoo's autonomy to be one of the assets that have contributed to its excellence. If the city ran the Zoo, it would be just one of a multitude of metropolitan concerns ranging from rapid transit to crime prevention to housing development. At the very least, it would have to compete with other park commission concerns for money and attention. Under the existing setup, decisions are based solely on what's good for the Zoo.

But enormous amounts of money are needed to sustain the operation of the Zoo. The moated enclosures that make it so beautiful are incredibly expensive—much more expensive than traditional wire cages. The Zoo sometimes spends more money on one enclosure than small zoos have in their entire annual budgets. Today the Zoo and Park together employ some 800 people, 500 of them full-time. In addition to the curatorial and veterinary staffs that work directly with the animals, such departments as accounting, personnel, purchasing, security, education, marketing, and maintenance are essential. In 1980, the annual budget for the Zoo and Park reached $26 million.

If the Zoo were funded by taxes, aggressive promotion might not be so important. But less than four percent of the annual budget comes from public funds. The city contributes just two cents of every one hundred dollars collected in city property tax to the upkeep of the Zoo— today that's just about enough to pay the water bill. Most of the Zoo's money comes from membership dues, admission fees, donations and sales of food, gifts, and tours.

Members of the Zoological Society of San Diego, who pay annual dues, are admitted free to the Zoo and Wild Animal Park and receive *Zoonooz*, the Society's monthly magazine. The Society currently has 89,000 members— the largest membership it's ever had, and the largest membership of any zoo in the world. Some three million people visit the Zoo every year, and another million visit the Wild Animal Park, and the admission fees from this gigantic attendance provide twenty-five percent of the annual budget. In addition, in the years since 1916, some generous individuals have made enormous donations to the Zoo. Still, sales of food and gifts, the guided bus tour and sky-ride at the Zoo, and the monorail train tour at the Park generate most of the funds with which we operate and build.

Zoos used to be quiet little parks that just took what moneys came in and did the best they could. But in the current tight economy, people pick and choose where to spend their money, and zoos have to compete actively for dollars. People have to be convinced that a zoo is worthwhile. That's where the job of goodwill ambassador comes in.

When the search for "Miss Zoofari" was announced in the papers, everybody in the Children's Zoo thought it would be a great job to have. Two hundred women applied, including me, though I didn't take my chances of getting the job very seriously.

The search for a representative went on for several months. The girl who was finally chosen was a model, and she was beautiful. But she couldn't drive, was nervous about public speaking, wasn't familiar with the Zoo or with the city of San Diego—and was ill-at-ease around many animals. Whenever she made an appearance, she had to be accompanied by someone who could drive, help handle the animals, and speak before a group.

After her year ended, the Zoo went for a couple of months without a representative, and there was considerable discussion about abolishing the job. Finally, the Zoo officials decided to hire another ambassador, but to choose someone with a more appropriate background.

The search for the second "Miss Zoofari" wasn't attended by as much hoopla as the first. The Zoo officials concentrated on applicants who had experience and on the girls who worked in the Children's Zoo handling animals. Like many of the attendants, I had helped the first goodwill ambassador during television appearances, and the Zoo director had liked the way I handled myself. So my original application was pulled and I was interviewed again, and in February 1970, I was named to the job.

I decided to drop down to part-time status in college for a year—I was a junior—then go back full-time, graduate, and go on to veterinary school. But as it turns out, I've still got the job as goodwill ambassador (though I banished the "Zoofari" label long ago) and I never did graduate. I just began to spend more and more time at the Zoo, as my job grew more and more demanding.

The Zoo really didn't make too much of my appointment, but the public-relations department did have the Zoo photographer take all kinds of pictures. One of the qualifications for "Miss Zoofari" was that she be photogenic, but the picture that ended up on the front page of the San Diego paper showed me holding a lion cub that had sunk its teeth into my chin and was tugging on my skin. It surely wasn't my best portrait, and things have not changed since then. I've posed for pictures with hundreds of animals, and it doesn't matter if I have one eye open and the other eye closed or if my hair is sticking up all over because the animal just swatted me in the head—if it's a good picture of the animal, that's what they use.

During my first weeks in my new job, I was a little lost. During my two years in the Children's Zoo, I had always had to be in a specific spot at a specific time—my morning and afternoon breaks were timed to the minute. Now I found myself in a vaguely defined job. I had to be available, but other than that, I didn't really know what I was supposed to do.

I began doing a tremendous amount of research to prepare myself in a general way. I spent hours in the library and hours locked in an office with piles of books. I memorized all the departments in the Zoo, learned the names of the major Zoo staffers, found out who to deal with at each level, and familiarized myself with the various animals and where they were located.

Because I wanted to be able to speak knowledgeably

about all facets of the Zoo, I studied its history. People who visit the Zoo as it is today—a sprawling landscape of canyons and mesas burgeoning with exotic plant and animal life—would probably find it difficult to imagine the Zoo's very humble beginnings in 1916.

It was in that year that Dr. Harry Wegeforth, a San Diego medical doctor, enlisted the cooperation of four friends, three of them also physicians, and founded the Zoological Society of San Diego. Their original collection was a small group of animals—a half-dozen monkeys, coyotes, and bears—left over from a menagerie at the 1915–16 Panama-Pacific Exposition in Balboa Park. Wegeforth took over these animals, which were kept in small cages not far from the Zoo's present entrance, and began soliciting the support of the citizens of San Diego in the form of money, materials, food, and animal donations, establishing the Zoo in the name of the children of the city.

"Dr. Harry" is a San Diego legend. He was an indefatigable—and apparently irresistible—fund raiser. He'd often go out and borrow money to buy animals, then confront well-to-do San Diegans with the fait accompli, saying, "Well, we bought these animals, so we *have* to come up with the funds to pay for them." He even persuaded wealthy citizens to loan their yachts for expeditions in search of animals.

Wegeforth had a wonderful sense of humor. During the early twenties, he approached John D. Spreckels, a San Diego theater owner, for help in paying the loan he'd taken to buy the Zoo's first two elephants. "I will, providing you can get whiter elephants than some I have now," the wealthy Spreckels replied, referring to some of his less successful business deals. The next day, Wegeforth bought a large keg of white powder and four of the largest powder puffs he could find and set the keepers to powdering the elephants. He then enticed Spreckels to visit the Zoo and led him to the elephant compound, where, as Wegeforth later recalled in his memoirs, "There stood the two snowy white bulging beasts, looking like nothing any mortal had ever seen, their black eyes and pink mouths the only spots of color in the large white expanse."

So appreciative of the joke was Mr. Spreckels that he immediately wrote the Zoo a check for $7,500—enough in those days to pay not only for the loan, but for the elephant compound.

Wegeforth used to love to ride through Balboa Park on his beautiful black Arabian stallion, occasionally dismounting to poke holes in the ground with his walking stick and plant seeds—the beginning of the botanical collection that is now considered one of the best in the world. He always loved plants, and as he traveled around the world on animal-collecting tours, he would fill his pockets with plant seeds to bring home. In the Zoo's early years, though he was still a successful physician with a busy practice, Wegeforth would go in person to beg fish from the waterfront vendors, plead with farmers for gifts of hay, and collect second-grade fruits and vegetables at the produce markets to feed the animals. Though he developed a reputation in the Zoo world as a shrewd animal trader and he traveled all over the globe in search of plant and animal specimens, he was also willing to stand at the Zoo gates and collect tickets.

For twenty-five years Dr. Harry defied politicians and courted voters in order to ensure the future of his Zoo. A few years after the Zoo's founding, he asked the City Council to allocate almost ten percent of the acreage of

Balboa Park to be its permanent home. When he met resistance from city officials and residents, he began to woo them one by one. As a result of his persistence, the city eventually decided to allocate the 128 acres that the Zoo now occupies, and the unique relationship between the Zoological Society and the city, under which the Society transfers ownership of all animals, equipment, and property, but retains managerial control, was established.

Wegeforth shaped every aspect of the Zoo's development, and his mark is evident today in many of its unique features. It was he who first envisioned a zoo spread over the rugged landscape, abounding with luxuriant trees and foliage from all over the world, and that vision required considerable imagination, for originally the Zoo's land was barren except for a few small eucalyptus trees left by a nursery that had leased part of Balboa Park. The huge flying cage for birds was one of Wegeforth's pet projects, and his interest in research into wild animal nutrition and diseases led to the establishment of the Zoo's hospital and laboratory facilities.

Wegeforth died in 1941. In a time when it was almost unimaginable for a woman to head a zoo, Belle Benchley, who had worked closely with Wegeforth for many years as the Zoo's executive secretary, took up his work and served as director until 1953. She published three popular accounts of her experiences, *My Life in a Man-Made Jungle; My Animal Babies;* and *My Friends, the Apes.* Mrs. Benchley is extremely well thought of in the zoo world and by the public at large, and everywhere I go, especially when I talk to senior citizens, people ask me about her.

She was succeeded by Dr. Charles Schroeder, a veterinarian, who was director when I started working at the

Zoo. Short, with a husky build, Dr. Schroeder is a man of determination and charisma. Like Wegeforth, he had a tremendous ability to elicit donations and involve citizens in the Zoo, and like Wegeforth, if Charles Schroeder wanted something, he wouldn't listen to the word "impossible."

Dr. Schroeder was outstanding at recognizing other people's efforts. After I became goodwill ambassador, he always took time to send me a note if he thought I'd done a good job at something. For all the power and pressures of his office, he had a flair for detail. Every morning, he'd walk from one end of the Zoo to the other with a notebook and jot down everything that needed attention, even a trash can that needed to be repaired, an area that hadn't been swept, or a post that was crooked.

Dr. Schroeder knew animals and was an outstanding fund raiser, a good businessman, and a good public-relations man. He was the force behind the Wild Animal Park, and under his leadership, the Zoo reached a new high in terms of reputation and support. Now retired, Dr. Schroeder travels all over the world and consults with other zoos. Wherever I go, Schroeder has been before, and people know and love him. It's incredible that people in so many places sing his praises.

As I studied, I realized that the efforts of the hardworking and committed individuals who built the San Diego Zoo are probably the most important ingredient in the Zoo's excellence. Harry Wegeforth, Belle Benchley, and Charles Schroeder went out and begged, borrowed, and virtually stole whatever they could to put the Zoo together. They had a lot of foresight, they knew where they wanted to go, and they had the drive to get there.

Changing times have brought increased specialization

to the Zoo. In her books, Mrs. Benchley told of her daily involvement with virtually every animal in the Zoo, but today's director, Chuck Bieler, couldn't possibly be intimately involved with all the animals. He has a $26 million a year business to run, and business acumen has become more essential to the post than knowledge of animals; animal expertise is more the province of the curators and vets and the people who work under them. Today we have one employee whose only responsibility is to keep up with all the legislation that affects the sale, transportation and maintenance of exotic animals, and instead of having one vet, the Zoo now has vets, pathologists, and behaviorists.

I had been chosen as goodwill ambassador primarily because of my animal handling experience. The Zoo had established a speakers' bureau, made up of members of the professional staff, to go out and get support for a $6 million general obligation bond needed to build the Wild Animal Park, and I used to accompany them with an animal. When I was introduced, I'd say a few words, but I was there primarily to transport and hold the animal.

I often went to events at which Dr. Schroeder was guest speaker. He was quite fascinating and was famous locally as a lecturer. He did a lot of talks and appearances, and he always liked to take animals along.

Dr. Schroeder began to ease me into public speaking. He'd introduce me, and the next thing I knew, he'd say, "Well, Joan, tell them about such and such." I'd be standing in front of a group of people, and it was sink or swim. I never knew what he was going to ask me to talk about, so I had to be up on everything that was going on at the Zoo.

In no time at all I was thrown into lecturing. The staff was getting more and more busy as the Park's opening drew closer, and since it was my job to represent the Zoo, I started giving speeches.

My first lecture, to a group of about forty men, was the first speech I'd ever given in my life. I just had to talk about the Zoo, but I was terrified. On the way to the hotel where I was speaking, the chimp that I'd brought along turned her cage over, and when we arrived, she was screaming at the top of her lungs. Then I discovered I'd brought the wrong box of slides. By the time I went back and got the right ones, I was late. The men were already seated at lunch, and when I walked into the banquet room, they all stood up. I wanted to die.

I was given a seat at the head table, which was elevated and faced all the other tables. Boots and short skirts were in style at the time, and I was wearing a white safari jacket, a white miniskirt and white boots. When the waitress came around with coffee, she filled my cup to the brim, and when I took a sip, I spilled it right down the front of my jacket. I was so nervous and ill-at-ease that I don't remember anything about the speech itself.

I started making local TV appearances, too, but they didn't frighten me very much. I would have been nervous if I had to go on television and talk by myself, but I always felt that I was just taking the animals on. I didn't feel very conspicuous.

In a short time I was on call for anything: conducting tours, lecturing, taking animals out in public, appearing on radio and television, and helping in the public-relations department, even stamping envelopes. Within a year, I was working a full schedule—nights, weekends, and holidays—whenever the Zoo called.

6

A Star Is Born

I soon had more requests for appearances than I could possibly handle, but my job still gave me some slack time when I didn't have any specific duties—I had given my lecture or made my appearance—so I could continue training Carol.

Red Thomas, who had worked as a keeper and had assisted the first goodwill ambassador during her appearances, was assigned to work with me as a handler. An easygoing man of medium build, with the freckles and red-blond hair suggested by his name, Red had worked with elephants before. Together we were able to really pursue Carol's training, because the two of us could position and hold her better than I could myself. One guy who worked in the Children's Zoo was always mimicking people, and his imitation of me was "Hi, where's Red?" because all the time I was out giving talks and making appearances, I couldn't wait to get back to the Children's Zoo, change into my Levi's jeans, find Red, and get back to work with Carol.

The three of us began to go everywhere together. Carol was at every opening in San Diego. We took her into restaurants, to a golf tournament, through a naval hospital, and into hotels, and she really became the star of the Zoo.

Carol was continually invited places because she could do things—hold signs, pose, give people rides, shake hands. A lot of exotics are interesting, but they don't do a whole lot. And Carol could go places because she'd been handled and disciplined and trained until she was very reliable, a rare quality in exotic animals. Now that I've worked with many more elephants, I appreciate how superior she was in terms of tractability. Around both adults and children, she was very gentle and eager to please.

Carol handled herself well in a lot of places where it seemed incredible to take an elephant, but she slipped up at a bank opening in Encinitas. The bank owners had decided it would be really neat to have animals from the Zoo at the opening, so I took Carol. They covered their brand-new carpet with a piece of plastic for her to stand on, but, as anyone who's ever been around elephants knows, when they urinate, it's a considerable amount of liquid. And unfortunately, like most exotic animals, they're most apt to do it when they get excited. The new bank was crowded and noisy, and Carol got nervous and let go an endless cascade that drenched an area far beyond the limits of the plastic sheet.

At that point, there was nothing I could do but apologize and help clean up. The way I look at it, if they want to have an elephant inside their new bank, they have to take their chances. They've got to figure that an elephant isn't totally potty-trained.

On another occasion, a health agency made a donation to the Zoo and we took Carol onto the patio of an office building at the Zoo for publicity pictures. I'd left some papers in my office, which was just inside the building, so I ran back for them, and Carol decided to follow. I swung the door open and walked through, and she came right behind me—but she got stuck halfway through. Our membership office was right inside the door, and people were standing in line to buy memberships. Two elderly women screamed and went running down the hall. They frightened Carol at least as much as she frightened them, and she deposited a load of dung right on the doorstep.

In order to be able to transport Carol, Red and I had to condition her to be at ease in a horse trailer. We'd put her in the trailer and put chains on her feet, feed her, and leave her for an hour. Then we'd let her out. We'd tell her to get in the trailer again, and if she didn't, we'd pull her in, feed her again, and leave her a while longer. We did it until she learned to go in and stand there without being nervous.

When we rode down the highway, Carol used to rock back and forth when she got bored, and the whole truck and trailer would jerk backward and forward. People in other cars would slow down to see what was going on, and then Carol would hang her trunk out of the side of the trailer. When people realized it was an elephant, they'd drive real slow alongside of us, so intent on watching what Carol was doing that they sometimes wouldn't watch what *they* were doing. I always worried that the police would stop us because we were distracting motorists.

❊   ❊   ❊

Red and I worked continually to learn more about elephant training. We used to search in the library for information. When circuses came to town, we'd go talk with the elephant trainers, and whenever we found somebody who knew more than we did, we'd get them to show us what they knew. But even though basic techniques have been developed for working different kinds of wild animals, and there are standard techniques for teaching an elephant certain behaviors, such as lying down, there's really no set way to teach an animal—particularly a wild animal—to do anything. You use trial and error till you find something that works. Training depends most of all on your ability to create a program through which you can communicate with an animal.

I soon learned that an important aspect of communication is understanding what may be frightening or strange to an animal. As before, it required putting myself in the animal's place—animals don't think with the logic of humans.

This fact was brought home to me when Red and I decided to teach Carol to get up on a pedestal. We put a big tub upside down in front of her, and the first time we asked her to, she jumped right up on it. The only problem was, once she got up there, she was terrified to get down. When she reached down with her front leg, she couldn't touch the ground. She had to actually let her weight drop forward in order for her foot to touch, and she wouldn't do that. She kept reaching down and stretching, first with one foot and then with the other, and even though she came within a couple of inches of the ground, she stood there and screamed and hollered and shook. I imagine she felt that if she put that foot all the way down she might fall forever, but we had just assumed that if she got up on a tub she would get down off a tub.

People all over the Zoo heard Carol screaming and came running to see what was going on. Red and I set out in search of a step stool that would hold an elephant, and finally came up with a sawed-off tree stump. We put it next to the pedestal and Carol stepped on that with one foot and then put the other foot on the ground and walked down off the tub.

We used a block and tackle to teach her to lie down. To train a dog to lie down, you position him with your hands. To train an elephant to lie down, you position her with ropes and a block and tackle, gradually stretching her legs apart until the easiest thing for her to do is lie down. You then hold her, say "Down," and reward her, repeating the training until she understands that she is to lie down and stay down until you allow her to get up. It's not abusive—you don't flop her down hard or jerk her legs out from under her, because that would frighten her, and she'd begin to associate "Lie down" with pain or fear. You're just showing her that when you ask her to lie down, this is what you want her to do. It's the only way you can be "big" enough to do that with an elephant.

The impact of the training goes far beyond teaching the elephant to lie down. For the first time in her life, she understands that a human being can physically restrain and control her and suddenly she looks at her trainers differently.

Sometimes training involves reinforcing a natural behavior to be done on command, and other times it's a matter of teaching an animal to do something that it would never do naturally. For example, an elephant picks things up with her trunk every day, but training is required to get her to do it when you tell her to. Walking around on her hind legs may or may not be a natural behavior for an elephant; elephants in the wild do stand on their hind legs if they want to get something that's high overhead. Standing on her forelegs is an unnatural behavior that an elephant can be taught to perform. Carol learned to stand on her hind legs and on her front legs on command.

When you're teaching an animal an atypical behavior, physical development becomes an important factor. An elephant couldn't possibly walk across a ring on its hind legs right off the bat. It might be able to take one or two steps, but to ask for more would be like asking an average person to do a perfect cartwheel or a ballet movement—it takes time to develop the musculature and coordination.

If Carol misbehaved or refused to do something she'd been trained to do, we'd discipline her with a slap of the hand or a jerk with the bull hook. It was comparable to spanking a child—Carol weighed a ton, so the amount of pressure and kind of discipline had to be adjusted accordingly.

For the first time, however, I began to encounter people who misunderstood and became outraged when they saw animals disciplined at all. Carol and Sumithi had been moved from the Children's Zoo to the main zoo, where they were kept in a small enclosure separate from the adult elephants, because they weren't quite old enough to live among them. One day Red and I were working with Carol there and she was being really obstinate, so we were smacking her and pulling her with the bull hook. She started screaming like a stubborn child because she didn't want to do what we were asking her to do, but we wouldn't give up; we were going to work her until she performed correctly. Not surprisingly, because elephants are very curious creatures, one of the adult elephants that was at the other end of the yard separated from us by a wall decided to see what was going on. As they like to do, she put her feet up on the wall and hung over the top, taking in everything we were doing. This was great entertainment—she had nothing better to do, and there was nothing more exciting going on in the Zoo.

A visitor walking by saw this scene quite differently. What she saw was that we were mistreating a baby elephant while its mother tried frantically to get over the top of the wall to save it. (One thing this woman didn't realize was that none of the elephants has a mother in the Zoo.) She wrote very abusive letters to the Zoo, calling me terrible names, and she also wrote to the Humane Society of San Diego and the National Humane Society.

I was tremendously upset. I've loved animals all my life, and here was this woman accusing me of mistreating a baby elephant!

That woman doubtlessly acted out of positive motives—she was concerned about Carol being abused—but, like people who call for the abolition of zoos, she didn't have the facts with which to evaluate the situation. Some Zoo people use the term "humaniacs" to describe people who carry their concerns about humane treatment of animals to an absurd extreme and cause a lot of unnecessary problems in the process. I understand the concern of these Zoo visitors, but I think their worry would be alleviated by a better understanding of our work.

The publicity generated by my appearances with animals contributes to the Zoo's survival, and therefore to the well-being and even the perpetuation of many species.

But each time I exhibit an exotic outside the Zoo, there is potential for harm to the animal or the people around it. I'm always aware of the risk, and so is the Zoo. In weighing the educational and public-relations value of any appearance against the inherent risk, the people in the PR department rely on my judgment.

I try to reduce the risk by conditioning animals in advance to be comfortable with sounds and objects that they may encounter outside their normal surroundings. When Red and I were training Carol, we took her to areas where there were trucks, and gradually got her used to crowds and all sorts of noises.

In July of 1971, I was invited to be in the annual Independence Day parade in Coronado, a San Diego suburb. They wanted me to ride in the back of a convertible holding an animal, but I had always thought that was silly, so I decided to ride Carol and carry an orangutan, Robella. I thought Carol would behave well, and she did, until an antique car, equipped with one of those horns that plays a tune, pulled up behind us.

The parade was almost ready to begin, and the streets, all closed to traffic, were lined with floats and bands and majorettes and horseback riders. Everybody was getting organized, starting their engines and getting in place, when the driver of the car sounded his horn. I'm sure it never occurred to him that he would frighten Carol; people often do things that frighten animals without realizing it. But the sound terrified her. She let out a scream and took off, running down the street with me on her back and the orang in my arms.

People started running and screaming. Carol was plowing through fences and hedges, oblivious of me and everything else, with Red Thomas close at her heels. I didn't even think about being scared. All I could think of was the orangutan, which was very valuable, and the people. I was worried that other people might get hurt, or that Carol would damage something and get in trouble.

When she headed for the side of a house, I jumped off with the orang in my arms. An elephant runs fast, but if you had the choice of jumping off a runaway elephant or going head-on into a house on top of her, you'd jump off, too. In her panic, Carol might well have rammed right into the wall, but she caught her foot in a ladder lying on the front lawn and fell. That kind of caught her attention. She realized that nothing was chasing her, and she calmed down. Red and I got her under control and walked her back to the trailer and took her back to the Zoo.

The next morning, we were called into the director's office. The owners of the fences and the hedges and the ladder had called and wanted to know if the Zoo was going to pay for them. But the people who ran the parade had called and said that they would pay for them, because they had invited us.

Though Carol was a trained performer, she was an elephant with the same instincts as any elephant. Yet one day when I was showing her, a man pushed a baby in a stroller right underneath her, between her legs. My heart was just pounding. As it happened, Carol stood quietly, and nothing bad happened. But public appearances are difficult just because bright lights, sudden noises, and crowds can frighten or confuse an animal.

Maury Cohen, who was under contract to make films at the Zoo and get them on news programs in Los Angeles, was a zealous PR man, pushing all the time to place stories. Once he sent me to a Los Angeles television station to appear on a local program. When Red and I arrived and told them we were from the Zoo, they said, "Oh, you're Miss National Wildlife!" I didn't know what they were talking about. "No," I said, "I'm Joan Embery from the San Diego Zoo." They let me in and I went on the show, but when they introduced me, they said I was Miss National Wildlife. It turned out that it was National Wildlife Week, and Maury had told them I was Miss National Wildlife. But he hadn't told me anything; I didn't figure out what was going on until I was on the air. The host said, "Well, Miss National Wildlife, since you work for the San Diego Zoo, what is your zoo doing in accordance with National Wildlife Week?" We weren't doing anything. I didn't know what to say, so I just kind of stood there a minute, and then I said, "Well, of course, we practice conservation every day."

Nonetheless, Maury and I got along well. In time, I thought Carol could do everything that an elephant had ever done and more, but one day, Maury was kidding me about her. "You know, Carol can't do everything yet," he said. "You ought to teach her to paint." He laughed, but I thought, "She can do anything; sure she could learn to paint," and I resolved to teach her.

I got a paintbrush, a big one like you use for a house. Carol could already pick things up, so all I had to do was tell her to pick up the brush. Then I'd take her trunk, still holding the brush, and swing it back and forth and feed her. I'd do this over and over, and then wait a few minutes. If I waited long enough, she'd start to move the brush out of boredom, and every time she did, I'd reward her, saying, "Good girl, paint." Then I'd sit there and say, "Paint." If she didn't swing the brush on her own, I'd move her trunk back and forth and say "Good girl" and reward her.

After I did it enough, she started to understand. Then I moved her to a more complex behavior. I laid a board in front of her, and if she swung the brush back and forth across it—not off in the bushes—I'd reward her. If she swung it off to the side, I'd tell her "No," bring her trunk back, and tell her to paint on the board. This technique— molding behavior by rewarding an animal for doing something that comes close to what you want and continually asking for something that's a little closer—is known among trainers as "training by approximation." In time, Carol learned to pick up the brush, dip it in a bucket of paint, swing it back and forth across the board, get more paint, and swing it back and forth again. When she finished, I'd press her trunk on the board to leave an imprint, then tell her to stand on it—and she'd put her foot on it and make a big footprint.

In the beginning, I'd say, "Pick up the brush—paint— put the brush in the bucket, pick it up—paint," but after she'd gotten the idea, I'd just tell her to paint. If she forgot to put the brush in the bucket, I'd tell her and she'd do it. We used a nontoxic paint that was easy for her to spread. Sometimes I'd put a little bit of each of three different colors on the board—just to increase the visual impact of the painting—and let her brush it around.

It took a few weeks of daily work to get the whole idea across to Carol, and a couple of months till she really started to get the hang of it and show some initiative about it. She thought it was great fun. She liked to work, and this was something interesting. Like most children, she liked to play in paint. Sometimes she was so eager that it was funny. People would crack up because she looked like she was having a ball, swinging the brush all over, putting it in the paint, and slopping it on the board.

I was so proud of what I'd done that I couldn't wait to show Maury. He thought it was fantastic and had still photographs and movies made of Carol painting to use for publicity. All kinds of magazine and newspaper articles were published, and Carol's painting became an incredibly popular attraction.

We gave her paintings titles like "Sunset at the Zoo," "Explosion," and "Pollution," depending on what the colors and shapes suggested. When we decided to sell them for $100 apiece, taking the money as donations to the animal acquisition fund for the new Wild Animal Park, we earned three or four thousand dollars. Carol had a "one-elephant show" at the Zoo one weekend.

Years before, when I'd started training Carol in the Children's Zoo, I had approached Dr. Schroeder about putting on shows with her, but he had turned me down. Though a trained seal show had been a regular Zoo feature for years, the Board of Trustees believed that the Zoo should maintain its image as a zoological garden, not a circus of trained animals.

But after Carol became famous far and wide for her painting, Red and I began doing shows with her in the Zoo's amphitheater, Wegeforth Bowl, as a special attraction on big holiday weekends. In a simple fifteen-minute show, she would paint and do her other tricks, and I'd demonstrate how we trained her.

The publicity surrounding Carol's painting led to my first appearance on national television, in October 1970, on "What's My Line?" The invitation, which came through the Zoo's PR department, meant flying to New York, so I just took along a film clip of Carol at work.

It was my first trip to New York, and I felt kind of lost in the big city. Someone at the Zoo had looked up the name of a hotel in a book and made a reservation for me, and I found myself in an ancient, fallen-down place in one of the sleaziest parts of Manhattan. There were red lights in the corridors, and I kept hearing people out in the hallways, knocking on doors. The first night I was there, I called a high school friend who had left San Diego to live in New York. "I don't think I like it here," I told her. "I feel very uncomfortable." When she found out where I was, she was flabbergasted. "No wonder!" she said. "My God, what are you doing over there?" The next day I moved into the Americana, a gigantic modern hotel in midtown Manhattan.

Because I didn't want the "What's My Line?" panel to guess my occupation, I tried to dress deceptively—I wore a pink lace blouse and a long burgundy velvet skirt, and I had my hair done in a very curly style. I was so nervous that I didn't know if I'd be able to talk. My local television experience was still limited, and now I'd be going in front of millions of people with no animal to draw attention from myself. I knew I'd have to sign in when I walked onstage, and I was even afraid I might blow that.

My segment began with the host showing one of Carol's paintings and saying that there was something odd about it that the panel was supposed to figure out. Before they got through, they did guess that it had something to do with animals, but not that the picture was painted by an elephant or that I was an animal trainer—and they were pretty good at guessing.

Carol's debut on national television came three months later, when she was invited to paint on "The Steve Allen Show," which was taped in Los Angeles. All year the excitement about our painting elephant just kept snowballing, culminating, in late 1971, in my appearance with

Carol, the wombat, Dudley Duplex, and Ken Orang on "Tonight."

Within a very short period, I appeared on several more national television shows. When I was on "Truth or Consequences" with Carol, I stood backstage with her on a piece of Astroturf, which was supposed to look like grass. When they opened the curtain and showed us, Carol stood there and pulled up Astroturf with her trunk. Supposedly, she was to be given as a prize, but of course it had been worked out in advance that she wouldn't really be given away. Still, I started to get a little worried, because the guy who won her decided he really wanted her. Luckily, his wife prevailed—she wanted the color TV.

7

The Orangs and I

Robella—the orangutan that Carol ran away with—was another animal that I took out frequently for lectures and TV shows. Robella had been born at the Zoo and raised in the nursery. Shortly before I started working there, she had graduated to the Children's Zoo, where she shared an enclosure with a chimpanzee. Another orang, Mary Fred, arrived a little later.

Orangutans, manlike apes that once ranged through Southeast Asia and today inhabit the swampy forests of Borneo and Sumatra, are physically adapted for living in trees. They have long arms—when they stand erect their hands hang almost to the ground—and their narrow feet and hands have hooklike fingers. Long red hair covers their bodies, and their broad faces are comic and expressive. Seeing the orangutans at the Zoo, sitting big-

65

bellied and affable, it's easy to understand why their name, "orangutan," means "man of the forest" in the Malay language.

Like most orangs, Robella was very easygoing and very methodical; she put a lot of thought into whatever she did. One day, the chimp was frantically chasing a butterfly, and getting very upset because every time it lit on something and she grabbed at it, it would fly away. The chimp was getting more and more frustrated, and she started to scream and holler as she chased the butterfly around. Robella just sat there watching with an expression that said she found the whole thing pretty boring.

It wasn't long before the butterfly landed right in front of Robella. For a moment, she sat and looked at it, and then, very slowly, she extended her hand, picked the butterfly up, squished it between her thumb and forefinger, and dropped it matter-of-factly to the ground. That was Robella for sure, and it's pretty typical of all orangutans.

Robella was second only to Carol in my interest, and to this day, I like orangutans and elephants best of all zoo animals. I especially like working with animals that have a high level of intelligence; they tend to be molded more by experience and learning than less intelligent animals. Like Carol, Robella had a lot of personality. She was independent, rebellious, and a bit difficult to handle at times, but I got along with her very well. Many of the other girls preferred Mary Fred, because she was more disciplined and usually did what she was told.

The orangs got to know the Children's Zoo routines quite well. Robella never wanted to go into her cage at night, and often threw a tantrum because she wanted to stay up and play. Mary Fred used to come down into the ape house, actually push Robella into her cage and close the door, like an older sister saying, "Okay, now you're going to go into your bedroom and go to bed," then go into her own cage and shut herself in.

Orangs are very mechanically inclined. They have strong, dextrous fingers, and they love to take things apart. One day, when I was still working as a Children's Zoo attendant, I was sitting in the ape enclosure showing the orangs to some children. I was feeding Robella her milk, and Mary Fred was there, too, so I was busy with both of them. All of a sudden, everybody started laughing. At first I thought they were laughing at the apes, but the laughter went on and on, till finally somebody whispered to me that Robella had completely unbuttoned my blouse.

Robella and Mary Fred dismantled the shade structure in their enclosure in a single day, even though it was held together by bolts. We couldn't believe they did it, but orangs think nothing of time. If a chimpanzee can't get something apart right away, he'll get frustrated, but an orang will work with endless patience until it finishes whatever it's trying to do.

Given a choice between taking an orang or a chimp out in public, I'd generally prefer the orang. Orangs are less excitable than chimps, which are often frenetic and temperamental, and they're also much more unusual. With their bright orange-red hair and the white areas around their eyes, they look great on television.

Robella had a couple of habits that added suspense to every appearance I made with her. She liked to pull women's nylons away from their legs—it just fascinated her that she could do that—and she liked to look up under their dresses. Miniskirts were popular when I worked with her, and more than once, when an unsuspecting woman was admiring this cute little orang, Robella would suddenly pick up her skirt and look underneath. If I wore a dress and stockings when I took Robella out, I had to be on guard every minute.

I handled Robella when she was between one and four years old, until she weighed about forty pounds. Orangs at the Zoo aren't usually handled past four years of age. Full-grown females weigh about 120 pounds; full-grown males, about 250 pounds. Because they live high in trees in the wild, they develop very powerful arms and hands and feet, and they sometimes bite. They're very strong even as infants, because in nature baby orangs have to be able to cling to their mothers as they move through the treetops.

I didn't train Robella to do tricks, but I did discipline her. She knew what I meant if I said, "Sit here" or "Be quiet," and if she didn't behave, I spanked her, like a child.

The animals I took to speeches and appearances had to learn to behave around people. At one luncheon, Robella was seated right next to me at the head table with the mayor and some city council members. The waiter brought her a little dish of fruit, and she was very good for quite a while. Then she decided to pour a glass of wine on one of the dignitaries. After that she didn't sit at the head table anymore.

She was often dressed up prettily when we went out. Since she sometimes had to wear clothes to keep warm, I thought she ought to look as appealing as possible (although dressing up the apes is frowned upon by many zoo people, partly because it encourages people to want them as pets). I used to go to babies' clothing stores to get outfits for her. After I had something picked out, I'd usually start worrying about the size, and the salesgirl would tell me it would fit a baby of a certain age, weighing a certain number of pounds. Then I'd tell her it was for an orangutan.

Robella was generally very well-behaved, but orangs are like children, always looking for things with which to entertain themselves. They get bored sitting in one place and want to take off and play, and they can be very destructive.

When I worked with Robella, I was still living at home with my parents and sisters. Often I'd save time before lectures by picking up an animal at the Zoo, then stopping at home to shower and dress on my way to where I was speaking. If it was a manageable animal, I'd let it out of its cage in the house while I got ready. Once I took Robella home and asked my sister Linda to keep an eye on her while I showered. "Just get her some fruit and keep her occupied for a few minutes," I told her.

My sister told me afterward what a hard time Robella gave her. First she took Robella into the kitchen, put her on a chair, and gave her a banana. Robella peeled it very slowly and methodically, and when she was done, she set the peel on the table, took one bite out of the fruit, and threw the rest on the floor. So Linda decided to try an Oreo cookie. Robella took that, screwed it apart, licked the icing off each side, and threw the cookie part on the floor.

I could hear Linda saying to Robella, "Now you stop this, that's not very nice. You sit down and behave. Stop that."

"Don't tell her to stop it—smack her," I yelled. So Linda gave Robella a little smack on the arm—and Robella reached over with her other arm and socked her back, really hard.

Then Linda took Robella into the living room and sat

her down in front of the television set, thinking that it would keep her occupied, as it does most little kids. But Robella jumped up, ran up to the TV, and began pounding on it, then she started swinging back and forth on the doors of the cabinet.

I was in the shower and soaking wet when Linda came running into the bathroom, yelling, "Come quick! Robella's going crazy!" She figured that Robella was going to break the TV and that my dad was going to get really mad.

I ran into the living room with a towel wrapped around me, grabbed Robella by the arm, and shoved her into a chair. "Now, you just sit there!" I yelled. And she just sat, like a perfect little angel, and didn't move. But in the fifteen minutes that my sister had been minding her, she'd torn the place apart and hit Linda twice. She was only about two feet high, but really strong, and she had Linda completely buffaloed.

That's how it usually was. Robella would behave while I was around, but the minute I'd leave the room, she'd get herself into trouble, and when I'd come back and yell at her, she'd give me a defiant smile. Orangs have blackish gums, very white teeth, and very big lips, and when Robella did things she wasn't supposed to do, she'd get a huge grin on her face.

In June of 1970, I traveled with Robella to Colorado and Arizona to make television appearances. We flew from San Diego to Denver and back to promote the inauguration of new airline service between the two cities, then turned right around and flew to Phoenix and Tucson.

Though many promotional pictures were made of Robella and me apparently about to get on the Denver flight together, she was actually shipped in the baggage compartment. It is against Federal Aviation Administration regulations to have animals in an airplane cabin unless they can be contained in a cage small enough to fit under a seat.

Although the baggage compartment is pressure and temperature controlled, conditions vary more there than they do in the cabin. I worry about that, and I worry because anytime an animal is out of my sight there's a possibility that it will be misplaced, left at the airport, or put on the wrong plane. I've heard of shipments of animals that went to the wrong destination—nobody knew where they were until a phone call came from the airport that found itself with a bunch of waylaid exotic creatures.

Often when I travel, I choose animals especially because they're small enough to fit under an airplane seat. Several—but not all—airlines will allow you to fly animals in the passenger section if they fit under the seat, provided you make arrangements in advance and there's no one else with animals on the flight.

The pilot generally has the final say about what can go on his plane in the passenger cabin, so even if the ticket seller, the person at the gate, and the stewardesses have let me through, even if I've cleared the animal with the airline in advance, the pilot can say, "No, I won't take that animal," at the last minute. Once I flew with an animal from the East Coast all the way back to Los Angeles, only to get grounded by a pilot who wouldn't let me on the twenty-minute flight to San Diego.

Before I take any flight with an animal, I always call the airline and explain that I want to fly an animal in a crate of a particular size. If the animal has to go in baggage, I lock the crate so no one can open it, and I give the airline personnel detailed notes telling where the animal's supposed to go and on what flights, and whom to contact at either end if problems arise.

The first thing I do when I get off a plane on which I have an animal in baggage is go to the desk and say, "I have a valuable animal on this flight. Where will you be taking the crate off the plane?" The airline personnel aren't always geared to transporting animals and they don't think about making them comfortable. To them, a cage is just one more bag in the hold, and at small airports, they frequently line up all the cargo outside, regardless of heat, cold, or rain. Twenty minutes in very hot or cold weather could kill some animals or put them in serious danger. In those conditions, I make sure the animal is brought into the airport, and I never ever make a plane change without checking to see that the animal is properly transferred.

The crate Robella traveled in had tiny air holes, about as big around as your finger, so that she couldn't get her arms out and get hurt. I used to put a pink blanket in the crate with her, and to amuse herself, she would tear strips off the blanket and poke them out the holes. When I traveled with Robella, I knew she hadn't been left behind if I could see a trail of pink blanket fuzz leading out to the airplane.

During our trip, Robella stayed in my hotel rooms. I always okayed that ahead of time, too. Otherwise I might find myself kicked out on the streets of a strange city with an orangutan, and anyway, it's pretty hard to smuggle a three-foot cage through a hotel lobby.

In Denver, the people who worked for the airline wanted to take me out to dinner. I really didn't want to leave Robella in the hotel room by herself, so they called the hotel baby-sitter. When she showed up, I said, "What you're going to be baby-sitting is my orangutan here—

she's in the cage. The phone is right there, and if you have any problems, here's a number where I can be reached." I warned her that she mustn't let the orangutan out of her cage, because I knew that anyone who didn't know how to handle animals would find it difficult to control her. The baby-sitter thought the whole thing was pretty amusing. She settled in to watch TV and she talked to Robella to keep her quiet. They shared a candy bar, and it worked out just fine.

Another night, when I came back to the hotel, just exhausted after a day of interviews, Robella didn't want to get into her crate. When I finally got her in there, she started running from one end to the other, jumping up and down, screaming and pounding on the aluminum sides.

I was tired, and I didn't want the racket she was making to create problems in the hotel, so I took her out of the cage, put her in bed with me, and held onto her arm, figuring that as soon as she'd fall asleep I'd put her in her cage. But I dozed off first, and Robella must have realized it immediately. I woke up suddenly to find the lights and television on, and Robella running around, climbing the sides of the bed and grabbing the light fixtures overhead. In a matter of minutes she had flipped every switch and grabbed hold of everything in the room. She was having a heyday.

Wherever we were staying, I'd go out and buy fresh fruit for Robella to eat. One afternoon in Arizona, I stopped at a fruit stand and bought a bunch of ripe cherries, and when I got back to my hotel, I sat eating them and throwing the pits in the wastebasket. I gave Robella a handful, which she ate as she sat on the bed. I walked out of the room for a moment, and all the time I was gone, I kept hearing a strange plunking sound. When I went back to Robella, she was still sitting on the bed, eating the cherries—and throwing the pits in the wastebasket.

When I took Robella on television shows, I took along food, usually a banana, to keep her occupied, so she wouldn't get bored and start grabbing things. People were always amused by her eating habits—she'd eat a little bit, stick her lower lip out like a little platter and inspect her partially chewed food, then put it back in her mouth and chew again.

On one TV show we did in Denver, we were sitting near a big artificial tree that was part of the set. I saw that Robella had her eye on it, so I kept a close watch on her, but just as we were about to go off the air, the woman hosting the show asked me a question and I was momentarily distracted. In a split second, Robella reached out one long arm, grabbed the tree, and pulled the whole thing over on top of the interviewer and me. The show ended with us struggling out from under.

Robella had hair about four inches long all over her body, and after a night in her cage, she was always a mess. The first thing I had to do each morning was give her a complete bath from head to toe—I'd wash her like any other kid with bath soap or shampoo—and afterward, I'd be badly in need of a bath myself. I couldn't put her back in her cage, because she'd get dirty again, and I couldn't let her go loose, because she'd tear the room apart. So I'd take my shower holding on to her with one hand and washing myself with the other.

Before a cocktail party given by the airline in Denver, one of the representatives of the Convention and Visitors Bureau, who was just fascinated by Robella, offered to help me bathe her. We put her in the tub, and I started washing her while he handed me the soap and tried to hold her hand. When she was all lathered up, I said, "Just keep an eye on her so she stays in the tub," and started into the other room to get a towel. I took only a couple of steps before Robella went flying out of the bathtub and landed in the guy's arms. He was in a suit and tie with Robella wrapped around him, soaking wet and covered with suds. I started laughing so hard that it was all I could do to help him with her.

Robella's cage was so big that it took two people to carry it, so when I took her to appointments, I just carried her in my arms like a baby. Before going out, I'd wrap her in a blanket and put it over her head. Even though hotels were cooperative about my keeping her in my room, I tried to be discreet. I knew some guests might not appreciate having an ape in one of the rooms, and other people, if they saw me, would think they should have the same privileges and be allowed to keep their pets with them.

One morning, on my way to a newspaper interview, I got on the hotel elevator with Robella, all wrapped up in her blanket, in my arms. The elevator was packed because there was a businessmen's convention in town, and a lot of the people in the elevator were still half-asleep. Suddenly Robella pulled the blanket off her head and looked up at everybody. Some of the people started cracking up, and others just stood there looking with total disbelief at this extremely strange-looking infant with red hair all over its body and white circles around its eyes. But Robella took it all in stride. She just looked at them as if to say, "What are all you guys staring at? We do this every day!"

8

Zoo Babies

The frequency of my talk-show appearances depends on the availability of unique, handleable animals. At various times, I've taken specimens from almost every part of the Zoo on TV, but most often, I handle babies from the nurseries or young animals that were raised in the nurseries and live in the Children's Zoo. They're the new attractions at the Zoo, and young animals always have a lot of appeal. Indeed, one of the pluses of my job is the opportunity to keep up with what's going on in the nurseries.

There are two nurseries in the Children's Zoo—the main nursery, for primates and cats and such, and the hoofstock nursery. Baby animals are hand-raised in them if for some reason their mothers are unable to care for them. A mother may die or neglect her baby. She may hold it and carry it around, but not let it nurse, or she may lack sufficient milk to nurse. If either mother or infant has an illness or injury requiring daily medical care, the baby has to be raised in a nursery; separating a wild animal mother from her baby is difficult, and it wouldn't be practical to do it day after day.

For reasons we don't yet understand completely, mother cats occasionally eat their young. If a cat eats her first litter, later litters are taken from her, provided keepers or other Zoo personnel are on hand when she gives birth. Newborn animals sometimes have to be removed from enclosures that hold many specimens because they are harassed by some of the adults. Occasionally, animals so young that they have to be hand-raised are brought to the Zoo. But considering the size of the Zoo, relatively few baby animals wind up in the nurseries.

Nursery work is the most sought-after job among the Children's Zoo attendants, who may be moved there after they've had some experience, provided they show an aptitude for that kind of work. The truth is that few people really have the stomach for feeding, diapering, and cleaning up after baby animals or the emotional stamina to face illnesses or deaths of infant charges.

The nurseries are busy around the clock. Many baby animals are fed every two hours, some even hourly until they begin to nurse. It's often a struggle when they first come in, because even though they need food, they don't know how to eat, certainly not from a bottle, and the attendants have to teach them.

Bottle, nipple, and food are all specialized for individual animals. Extremely small marsupials drink out of catheter tubes attached to a syringe; the apes drink out of regular baby bottles, and an elephant's bottle has a

I also had the chance to show
Johnny's television audience Dudley
Duplex, one of the Zoo's two-headed
California king snakes, produced
as the result of an incomplete
twinning process. The other snake
shown here was known as Nip
and Tuck. In nature, two-headed
snakes are short-lived, perhaps
because the heads compete
for prey, making the snake an
inefficient predator.

Carol the painting elephant was the featured
performer the first time I ever appeared on "The
Tonight Show" with Johnny Carson, in 1971.

Ken, a young orangutan also known as Boom Orang, was also along that first night, and he
captivated Johnny and Ed McMahon.

The San Diego Zoo's worldwide reputation is based in large part on the number of exceedingly rare species that it has successfully maintained. Among them are Indian rhinoceroses, of which there are only 1,100 in existence. The Zoo's pair of Indian rhinos didn't breed for years, but shortly after the 1972 opening of the Wild Animal Park, the Zoo's open-space breeding annex, they bred. Gainda, a 120-pound female calf born in 1978, was the first infant to survive. The Metro-Toronto Zoo once paid $120,000 for a pair of Indian rhinos, one of the costliest animal acquisitions on record.

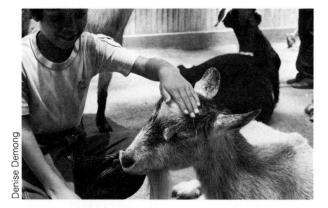

Denise Demong

Left: For youngsters, coming face to face with a goat or sheep can be even more thrilling than seeing the more rare Zoo animals from a distance. In the paddock of the Children's Zoo, they have that opportunity.

Below: The San Diego Zoo is noted for its beautiful park setting and its moated enclosures, which eliminate the need for cages. Buses carry Zoo visitors on guided tours over the hilly terrain.

This young African Southern white or square-lipped rhino, one of more than thirty raised at the Wild Animal Park, was probably the first rhinoceros ever to appear on live television.

Though the San Diego Zoo had two kiwis—nocturnal and flightless birds from New Zealand—for years, they had no luck getting them to breed. Like many birds, kiwis lack sexual dimorphism—males and females look alike—and when the Zoo's research department developed a technique for sexing birds by measuring the hormone levels in their fecal matter, it was learned that both specimens were males. Since then, two females have been acquired.

The Zoo has three Komodo dragons, the largest lizards in the world, which grow to a length of about ten feet and weigh as much as 365 pounds. They have sharp claws and teeth, and in the wild they prey on goats, hogs, and deer. By the early 1960's, the total world population of Komodo dragons was only about 300.

Perhaps no animal is more closely identified with the San Diego Zoo than the koala; San Diego is the only zoo outside of the animal's native Australia that has them. Koalas are nocturnal and feed on the leaves of eucalyptus trees, which are abundant on the Zoo grounds.

After his mother died, Gum Drop, a young koala, needed continual attention, so Jane brought him home to stay with us for a few months. Gum Drop was a quiet animal, but occasionally he liked to play with the dogs, especially my beloved Springer spaniel, Brave.

Also rare in zoos are okapis, which are native to Zaire. Though the stripes on their lower body are reminiscent of zebras, they are in fact members of the giraffe family. Their purple tongues are so long, they can clean their own ears with them.

When I was first named Miss Zoofari, one of the main demands of my job was to look pretty in pictures with the Zoo's animals. I wore this Santa suit for three Christmases, here for a portrait with a sea lion, till I finally put my foot down.

I felt more comfortable when the suit was on this young orangutan, though his thoughts on the subject were never recorded.

When one views the lush 128-acre Zoo today, it's difficult to imagine its humble beginnings in 1916. In the Zoo's earliest days, these spare wolf cages lined Park Boulevard, a block from the Zoo's present location.

Dr. Harry Wegeforth was the Zoo's founder and the driving force behind its growth and excellence for some twenty-five years. Dr. Harry liked to take a break from his medical practice to ride through the Zoo grounds on his Arabian stallion.

Everything seemed under control when my father snapped this shot of me before I was about to appear in a Fourth of July parade riding Carol and carrying Robella the orangutan. But a moment later, the driver of an antique car behind us sounded his horn, terrifying Carol, who took off at a full run. Red Thomas, at right, shared the work, if not the glory, during my first years as the Zoo's goodwill ambassador.

Robella had an outgoing personality and always enjoyed being among people. Here, at about 2½ years of age, she charms a group of young Zoo visitors.

In 1970, Carol had a "one-elephant" show at the Zoo. When we sold her paintings for $100 each, we raised more than $3,000 for the animal acquisition fund for the planned Wild Animal Park.

Above: Carol made her national television debut on "The Steve Allen Show." Though she was only half-grown, Steve was reluctant to get close to her—or perhaps he feared she'd paint him right along with the canvas.

Below: Robella, like all orangutans, liked to chew her food a bit, then make a platter of her lower lip and inspect what she was eating. Her distinctive eating habits fascinated Virginia Graham and her audience when we appeared on "Girl Talk."

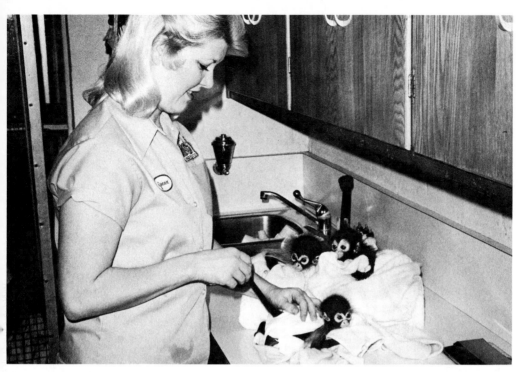

Above: JoAnn Thomas, head of the Zoo's main nursery, diapers three young spider monkeys. She uses regular disposable diapers—with holes cut in them for the tails to go through.

Below: "Our Gang" at the nursery in early 1979. At left are Lock and Lisa, one of only five sets of twin orangutans ever born in captivity. The animals at center and right are pygmy chimpanzees, which are among the rarest of Zoo animals. The young orang between the chimps is Robella's first infant.

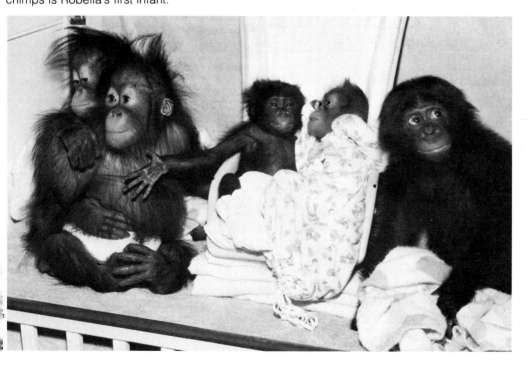

A step stool is often required for bottle feeding babies like this. This giraffe, 5'7" at birth, was raised in the Care Center at the Wild Animal Park.

It seems hard to imagine any mother abandoning a baby like Jim, but Dolly, a lowland gorilla at the Wild Animal Park, was raised in captivity, and when she gave birth to Jim, he was the first baby gorilla she'd ever seen. She resisted all his attempts to cling to her, so he had to be raised in the Park Care Center.

When Dolly became pregnant a second time, a student from San Diego State University, using a handmade doll and food rewards, undertook to teach her how to mother. And when Binti, a female, was born, Dolly raised her successfully. It is now hoped that other female gorillas at the Wild Animal Park will learn from Dolly's example.

This orphaned male American black bear was turned over to the Zoo's care by the Fish and Wildlife Service. It's a great challenge to work with bears. They bite and it takes constant work to accustom them to being held.

His name is Lovebug. A hand-raised leopard cub from the Tucson Zoo, he was only a few weeks old when this picture was taken. But he was already a handful, and he was upset by the photographer.

First stop in the NBC studios before "The Tonight Show" is Hair and Makeup. When Doc Severinsen's there, it's a chance to chat about our common interest in horses.

Above: Minerva the aardvark, also known as Krinkles, was raised in an incubator at the Zoo. Here she is on "The Tonight Show."

Below: Though harmless, the bearded dragon is ferocious–looking—when it feels threatened, it opens its jaw and inflates the "beard" of spiny skin across its throat. It took many days of practice for me to overcome my fear so that I could take one to "Tonight."

Johnny Carson kept his cool when I took a twelve-foot boa constrictor on the show, but the man whose job it was to open and close the curtain jumped so far out of my way as I walked offstage that he ended up rolled up in the curtain.

Transporting animals to television studios is often a major challenge. We needed a forklift to load this 500-pound Galápagos tortoise for the trip to Los Angeles.

Rowdy the llama is a seasoned traveler. When we took him to the "Dinah!" show, he readily jumped up into the carry-all, then slept with his head on my feet for most of the trip.

Above: When television programs tape on location at the Zoo, we can display animals that are too rare, too large, or too fragile to transport to a studio. We don't like to subject our koalas to the stresses of travel, but when the "Dinah!" show visited the Zoo, we were able to take the audience right into the koala enclosure. McLean Stevenson is at left, and between him and Dinah Shore is Jane Meier, one of the Zoo's veterinarians, with whom I shared a house for several years.

Left: Though she looks like a snob, Daphne the emu is really quite sociable. She's been seen by millions of Americans, in appearances on "The Mike Douglas Show," "Dinah!" and "Tonight." The emu, native to Australia, is the second largest bird after the ostrich. Emus are flightless, but are good swimmers, and they can run forty miles an hour.

Below: We could never have taken this twenty-two-foot Burmese python to a television studio. Indeed, several experienced reptile handlers literally had their hands full when the equipment broke down for half an hour during taping of "The Mike Douglas Show" at the Zoo.

Above: Many species are more likely to breed in captivity when they are free to range over large areas, as they are at the 1,800-acre Wild Animal Park. Visitors view animals from a monorail that runs silently on rubber wheels.

Below: During summers at the Park, the animals are most active in the cool evenings. Nairobi Village is illuminated and amber lights on the monorail permit night viewing with minimal disturbance to the animals.

San Diego Zoo Photo

Left: Among the animals the Zoo was unable to breed successfully until the opening of the Wild Animal Park are cheetahs. By late 1978, thirty-six cheetahs were born at the Park.

Below: The Arabian oryx is believed by some historians to be the source of the unicorn myth, because when it is viewed in profile, its long, slightly curving horns appear as one.

nipple that looks like a hose; sometimes it is a hose. Feeding the baby animals the diets devised for them by the Zoo vets is a complicated job. The sanitary system used for mixing formulas and filling bottles for the cats is the same system used for human babies in hospital nurseries.

Attendants have to change diapers on the apes, administer medications, bathe animals, and clean their cages. Baby cats don't even know how to go to the bathroom in the beginning, so the attendants have to rub their bottoms with warm water to relax them, accomplishing the same thing the mother cat does by licking her babies.

Those few baby animals that are extremely ill or that aren't expected to live are kept out of public view, but all the healthy babies in the main nursery are tended in a glass-walled room so Zoo visitors can see them. It looks much like a child's nursery. The baby apes wear diapers and sometimes pajamas, and the animals are kept in cribs and playpens and play with baby toys. The Zoo sometimes gets criticized for the human trappings of this environment, but there are reasons for all of it.

The diapers—regular disposable baby diapers with a hole cut in them to accommodate a tail—are for cleanliness; the pajamas, for warmth. Cribs, with their movable sides, happen to be convenient containers that keep babies elevated and away from drafts, regardless of whether the babies are humans or animals. When an animal gets large and strong enough to climb out of his crib, a top is attached.

Blankets in the cribs and playpens are surrogate mothers. Wild monkeys, in particular, are very dependent on their mothers, and their survival depends on their ability to cling to them. When they are raised in captivity, they get very neurotic if they don't have something to hold on to. Since the girls in the nursery can't sit and hold the monkeys all day long, they're given soft toys and blankets.

Toys also give the babies something to do—it's important to stimulate them physically and mentally so that they develop normally. A relatively recent addition to the main nursery is a television for the monkeys and apes to watch. Television was first used at Yerkes Primate Institute in Atlanta, Georgia, to overcome some of the boredom of primates in captivity. The set in the nursery is on for several hours a day, and the apes especially like to watch cartoons, soap operas, game shows, and animal shows while they play and explore in their pens. It may be that they respond to the soaps because of the emotional intensity of the actors' voices—certainly apes can sense distress, anger, happiness, or approval in human voices. Once, when an actor was weeping, a baby chimp actually climbed up and reached out to the screen.

The main nursery has been headed for many years by JoAnn Thomas, who started working in the Children's Zoo right before I did. JoAnn has a real gift for handling and feeding and giving animals a good start on life, something that requires a lot more than sticking nipples in their mouths. It's an incredible task to get an animal that doesn't want to eat—and doesn't know how to eat because it's never nursed before—to suck on a bottle. Baby animals may fight a bottle continually, even if they're starving to death. If an animal isn't eating right, JoAnn may take it home and get up every two hours all night long to feed it. It takes patience and fortitude to hang in and work with an animal, knowing that there's a very good chance it will die. It may die tonight or tomorrow night, or you may work with it, staying up night after night with it for weeks, and then lose it.

It can't be easy for someone as dedicated and involved with her animals as JoAnn is to hand them over to me to show in public. But over the years she's been very co-operative about my taking animals out of her care.

The Zoo's nurseries are intended to provide the very best care and insure the survival of as many of the Zoo's animal babies as possible. But there's no question in any Zoo people's minds that it's most desirable for each baby to be raised by its mother as it would be in nature. While every effort is made to provide optimal care in the nurseries, equal effort is made to give each animal mother the best possible chance of successfully caring for her own young.

Robella was raised in the Children's Zoo nursery because she was abandoned by her mother, a common problem with the great apes—gorillas, chimps, and orangutans—in captivity. The great apes are the largest and most human-like, and like humans, they spend the first years of life learning to do the things many other animals do instinctively. In nature, they learn how to take care of their offspring by growing up in a family, being taken care of by their mothers, and seeing other mothers care for their young. Apes raised in zoos often abandon their infants because they don't know how to mother.

It's important to get more mother apes to care for their own young so fewer babies will have to be exposed to continuous human influence in the nursery and Children's Zoo. Any time they're involved with humans, apes tend to take on human qualities, and the transition to living among other apes can be difficult.

A few years after I worked with Robella, a research project was developed at the Wild Animal Park to teach

Dolly, a female Western lowland gorilla, to hold and care for her baby. Captured at the age of nine months in western Africa, Dolly had never seen a baby gorilla until, at the age of almost ten, she gave birth to Jim on October 15, 1973. He was a healthy infant—at six pounds, four ounces, the largest gorilla ever born in captivity. (Gorilla infants are generally smaller than human infants at birth, even though males reach a weight of 500 to 600 pounds—females about half that much—as adults.) Dolly repeatedly resisted Jim's attempts to cling to her, and after six hours, when he showed signs of being cold, he was taken from her cage to the Wild Animal Park nursery, where he was raised.

The first viable captive gorilla birth ever recorded occurred in 1956 at the zoo in Columbus, Ohio. By early 1975, 105 gorillas had been born in captivity, but about ninety percent of them were separated from their mothers during the first or second day of life, and still, roughly thirty percent lived less than two weeks.

Within a few months of Jim's birth, Dolly became pregnant again. (The separation of infant apes from their mothers often results in the mothers becoming pregnant again within a few weeks, while females in the wild who rear their infants usually don't mate again until their youngsters are about three years old and have gained some independence. Frequent births take a toll on the mothers' health, another reason to get mother apes to care for their own young.)

When Dolly became pregnant for the second time, Steve Joines, a student at San Diego State University, began to train her. First he showed her movies of apes caring for their young, but when Dolly paid little attention, he resorted to training her with a handmade canvas doll with eyes, nose, and mouth drawn on in ink. Though gorillas are very tractable under controlled conditions, they are dangerous because of their apparent inability to judge their own strength, so Steve worked with Dolly through the bars of her cage, rewarding her with soybeans or apple slices when she performed correctly. It took her two or three days to learn to follow each of four commands: "Pick up the baby"; "Show me the baby"; "Be nice to the baby"—meaning Dolly should hold the doll to her breast and pat it—and "Turn the baby"—if Dolly were to hold the doll upside down or with its "face" away from her. Training sessions, conducted daily through the duration of Dolly's pregnancy, lasted about three hours, with long rest periods because of Dolly's limited attention span. Every day, Jim, who was seven months old when the project was begun, was brought to an area outside Dolly's "bedroom" where she could see him through the bars and observe people holding him and playing with him.

Dolly's baby—a female, Binti—was born about a year after Jim, on October 2, 1974, and Dolly began caring for her immediately, gently holding her close to her body at all times. Only the baby's crying confused her, but if someone said, "Be nice to the baby," Dolly would hold Binti to her and quiet her. After several weeks, she no longer required human prompting, and she successfully raised Binti herself. One of the great hopes of those involved in the research project is that her mothering will serve as an effective example for other female gorillas at the Wild Animal Park.

9

Stage Mother
to a Menagerie

Our first "Tonight" spot with Carol played so well that just three months later, in February 1972, I was asked to do another show. Craig Tennis, the talent coordinator, came to the Zoo beforehand, and I showed him around. When I took him through the education department, he spotted the tarantula we had there. It was about four inches long, with silky hair and long, fuzzy legs. "This is great!" Craig said. "You have got to take this on the show!"

I was horrified. I've never liked spiders or any kind of insects—I have almost a phobia about them. I had felt the same way about reptiles when I started working at the Zoo, but now I enjoy working with them. But I've never been able to get over the deep, innate revulsion I feel for spiders and insects.

I get the creeps thinking about that tarantula even now,

but Craig wouldn't take no for an answer, so I agreed. I thought that the show was important enough to the Zoo that I ought to do it, and even more, I felt that it was stupid to be as frightened as I was. I knew that the tarantula wasn't going to hurt me—contrary to popular belief, the tarantula's bite, though poisonous, is relatively harmless to people. I wanted to overcome my fear.

The tarantula was kept in a clear plastic shoebox with sand in the bottom and holes in the top. With the show about two weeks away, I put the box on my desk in the PR department and let it sit there for at least a week, maybe longer, while I tried to bring myself to pick up the tarantula. Just having it around almost drove me crazy.

First I tried to get used to the tarantula by just looking at it. After a while I was able to take the top off the box and put my hand inside, but every time the tarantula came near me, I'd jerk my hand out. Day after day I'd put my hand into the container and pull it out again. At last, when I had only a few days left, I got so I could let the tarantula crawl onto my hand. But I was afraid to push it off—I just had this fear that it would bite me—so I'd kind of throw it down. I didn't want to hurt it, but I could tolerate it only to a certain point and then my whole body would say no, my mind would just blank out, and I'd have to drop it. Everybody in the office was yelling at me: "You're going to smash that thing!" "You're never going to make it on the show with that thing!"

But I did it. I brought the tarantula onstage in its box, and Johnny and I sat and talked about it for a moment. Then I put my hand in the box and let the tarantula crawl onto my palm. I hated handling it so much that I was almost shaking, but I assured Carson that it wouldn't hurt him at all—if he would put his hand next to mine, the tarantula would crawl onto his palm.

I don't think Johnny realized how nervous I was. They shot a close-up of the tarantula crawling on his hand while he asked, "Do these things bite?" "Not unless you irritate them," I told him. Carson widened his eyes with mock terror, then looked at me deadpan and asked, "What irritates them?" "Blowing on them," I said. "Poking at them." Then Johnny really played it up—"Don't blow on it! Don't anybody breathe!" He was so much more at ease about the tarantula than I was that I let him put it back in the box.

For some reason, people like to think that Johnny Carson's afraid of animals, but I laugh when I hear that, because he's incredible. Fearless. I don't know of another person who would do some of the things that he's done on the show. He will hold any animal I offer to him—he relies on my judgment—and he's in very close proximity to every animal I bring on the show, even the more dangerous ones.

People relate to the spots I do with Carson because he gets involved and handles the animals, and he seems to really enjoy them. Carson is known for doing a reaction type of comedy—playing off whatever is happening at the moment—and it works especially well with animals, which are always unpredictable.

As it turns out, the tarantula spot was just the second of nearly forty appearances that I've made with Johnny Carson as of this writing, and in recent years, I've also been on "The Mike Douglas Show," "Dinah!" and a variety of other national shows with increasing frequency.

Healthy, happy, interesting animals are always a success on television. The San Diego Zoo has such a large collection that we can show creatures that have never been viewed on television before. People often write and say, "I've never seen an animal like that," or "I love the animals you pick because I never know what you're going to bring." When Johnny Carson introduces me on "Tonight," he often says, "Oh, I don't know what we've got backstage; let's see what Joan brought this time." And usually he really doesn't know. He and other hosts rarely see the animals before they come out on camera. I only work with them in advance if they're going to be involved in some way in a special act. When Carol—by then a very sizable elephant—made a return visit to "The Tonight Show" in 1976, she lifted Carson in her trunk. We made sure he practiced with her a couple of times before we taped.

My television appearances have public relations value, and they have monetary value, in the sense that the Zoo couldn't afford to buy the same publicity. But for me, their greatest value is educational. More people watch one "Tonight" show than visit the San Diego Zoo in a year's time. I've taken over 300 animals to the show (and never had one injured), and each appearance has given me the opportunity to tell millions of people that the animal that they're looking at may well be gone from the wild within the next few years. People must be made aware of the destruction of wild habitats so that they'll do something to preserve them.

Commercial animal trainers rent their animals for a fee—$250 buys you a tiger for four hours. The Zoo doesn't charge to take animals on television, and we pay our own expenses. In exchange, we expect recognition for the Zoo's efforts and we expect people to learn something from the spot. I've been very disgusted at times when I've taken animals on television and a host has been more interested in the fact that an animal was chewing on his shoe or piddling on the floor than in the fact that this is a spectacular example of a rare animal that leads a fascinating life in its natural environment, and whose very existence is threatened.

The Zoo is a serious, educationally oriented institution, but if we confined ourselves to participation in educational television shows, we'd reach a limited audience. To reach the larger group that watches entertainment-oriented shows, we have to adapt to the medium. Funny incidents often happen when I take animals on television, and that's fine with me, as long as I also have the chance to communicate what I think is important. If nobody learns anything about an animal, I go away feeling empty, because I haven't done my job—and sometimes I haven't been given the chance to.

Appearances on any of the national talk shows involve a tremendous amount of preparation. When I'm invited to do a spot on one, I first find out what new—newborn or newly acquired—animals are available at the Zoo. If it's a show I do regularly, I avoid taking on a species that I've shown recently, unless I'm taking a young animal on for the second time to show how it has grown. I try to come up with something different all the time, but of all the animals that the Zoo displays, ninety percent can't be taken to shows because they're never handled, not even by their keepers, who just work around them. Only certain species produce young on a regular basis, and infants of those species that raise their own young without difficulty rarely wind up in the nurseries, so they usually aren't available.

I have to think in terms of audience appeal. Some animals look great on TV because of their brilliant colors. The primitive primates called ruffed lemurs are terrific because they have large eyes, long tails, and long hair, black and white, in a truly beautiful pattern (the pattern is thought to camouflage the animal by breaking up its form visually). Some animals are more likely to be active than others. Cats are very popular, and baby apes are always great because they seem so much like human children. Many of the reptiles are fascinating; although many people don't like them, they like to see them, and to see someone handle them.

Once I offered to take an Arabian oryx, a type of antelope that is one of the Zoo's rarest and most valuable animals, actually extinct in the wild, to a television show, but the talent coordinator turned me down. "Oh," she said, "we've had antelopes on before." They really don't do a whole lot, she said, and that's true—many zoo animals don't do a lot because they aren't trained. From a talent coordinator's point of view, an antelope wouldn't show as well as some other animals.

I have to choose animals that are safe to handle and can withstand the trip to L.A., where most of the talk shows are taped. If it's summer, they have to have a tolerance for heat, and if it's winter, for cold. I search for a happy medium—a resilient animal that has lots of appeal and isn't going to be dangerous.

I consult with everybody—the Zoo's veterinarians, the curators, the department heads, the PR department, and the Children's Zoo staff director. I walk through the Zoo grounds and talk to the keepers to see if animals that I think would show well on television might be able to go.

The vets have to clear just about every animal that I take out of the Zoo, and I often have to get the agreement of JoAnn Thomas or "Boo" Shaw, who heads the hoofstock nursery, to take baby animals from their areas. (Boo—her real name is Kirstie, but everyone calls her Boo—started at the Children's Zoo about the time I did, and like JoAnn, she's been a big help to me over the years.) I also need the agreement of the appropriate curator. Sometimes a keeper has a say, if he's the one person who's worked with an animal all along, and in rare cases the Zoo director gets involved—if there's a difference of opinion about whether an animal should go, for example.

If anything happens to an animal, a lot of people have to answer for it, and as far as some of them are concerned, there's little to be gained by my taking a valuable animal like a pygmy chimp or a koala on television. I have to work with many people, and if any of them doesn't like me, doesn't feel I'm competent, or doesn't want a particular animal to go—if only because it's a risk he feels he has no reason to take, because he doesn't care whether we do a TV show—I can't do my job. I have to rely on a lot of people.

Sometimes I have to be very persuasive to get the animal I want. If I feel that an animal is good for show purposes and won't be harmed in any way, I'll push to get it, because if we don't come up with good animals, we won't keep getting invited to do shows. But I try to recognize valid reasons for refusing to let an animal be taken on television, and I try very hard not to argue with people over animals. My relationship with the people with whom I work every day is more important than any one television show.

There's a lot of paper work to do. I have to reserve a vehicle, request a cash advance to cover expenses, take out a Zoo credit card, and write memos to the departments involved, telling them when I'll be picking up animals and whether I'll need any assistants to go with me for the day. Sometimes I have to rent a special vehicle or arrange to take some kind of trailer.

If I'm taking nursery animals, which must be fed around the clock, I have to find out what food has to be taken along. Quite a few animals eat fresh fruit. If formulas have to be mixed, we do it ahead of time. Depending on the animal, a bottle may contain evaporated milk, KMR (cat milk replacer) or—for the apes—a formula called Esbilac. We have to take a cooler so the food doesn't spoil, and a warmer, to heat it before feeding it to the animals. We stop and warm the bottles at gas stations or restaurants.

A few days before a TV guest appearance, I start researching the animals I'm going to take on and discuss them over the phone with the talent coordinator of the show. Based on our conversation, he prepares a simple script. After I find out what aspects of the animal he thinks will be the most interesting to talk about, I dig up additional information. My goal is to be able to come up with an appropriate answer to any question a host asks. I bring home stacks of books, using as many as ten references for each animal and photocopying everything I find for my files. For some animals I'm lucky to find even a single reference, and for others, there are abundant sources, but they contain conflicting information that I have to resolve with keepers or curators.

I have to plan my outfit. While the Zoo pays my travel expenses for shows, I buy all of my clothes, and I spend a lot on them, because I want to project a good image. But often after I wear an outfit on TV I have to wear it only for handling animals, because it gets stained or the animals snag it with their claws.

I am paid for my appearances, and I've been a member of AFTRA, the American Federation of Television and Radio Artists, for many years. Under the Taft-Hartley Act, a performer or guest is allowed to do national television shows for one month without joining a union, but if you do shows in more than one month, you have to join. You don't even ask to join—all payments for shows go through AFTRA, and when it's time for you to become a member, they enroll you and send you a bill for the balance of your $300 initiation fee.

Before shows, I discuss crating and shipment with a veterinarian or the person in charge of the department from which I'm taking an animal. I have to find crates of the right size and construction. Some birds can't be put in wire cages because they might break their beaks or feathers. For them, I need plastic or solid wood cages. Sometimes cages have to be padded with foam or bedding or special crates have to be built. Some animals do better in cages that aren't solid, because if they can see they don't feel so confined. Sometimes an animal has to have a cage in its enclosure for a week so that it can walk in and out and eat in it and get used to it.

Taking a southern white rhino on "The Tonight Show" in February 1973 involved more preparation for moving an animal than any show before or since. We built a special crate to which we could attach a steel playpen, separated from the crate by a guillotine-type sliding door.

We got the rhino into the crate, winched it up into the back of an enclosed trailer for the trip to L.A., then winched it down again onto a dolly, transferred the rhino into the playpen, and rolled it onstage. It was the only way to show the rhino, since even babies are too big to pick up. This one was about four feet long, and if it started running, no one could stop it.

We took along a vet and one of the biggest crews that's ever accompanied me—six or eight people all together. The Zoo is willing to go to a tremendous amount of trouble and expense to insure that an animal can be displayed safely.

The night I took the tarantula to "The Tonight Show," Benny Kirkbride, who's run a daily sea lion show at the Zoo for 32 years, also came with some sea lions. He hauled them to L.A. in a portable tank—a covered pool that he had built to fit a trailer hauled by his truck. He could fill it partially with water for the trip, then fill it the rest of the way after he arrived.

Props and equipment all have to be taken care of before shows. If I'm showing a snake or a tree-dwelling animal, I may take a tree to the studio. Occasionally we need rather elaborate equipment, as we did when I took a young wallaby to a "Mike Douglas Show" taped in Las Vegas. The wallaby is a marsupial, like a kangaroo, and an infant normally stays warm in its mother's pouch, but this one was being raised in the nursery because its mother had died. It had to be kept in an incubator, though it could be taken out and shown for short periods of time. Mike's staff arranged to borrow an incubator from a Las Vegas hospital, and had it plugged in backstage when we arrived.

In addition to planning how to get animals from the Zoo to the television studio, I have to think about how I'm going to get them on- and offstage. When we took a Prze-walski's horse, the wild ancestor of our domestic horses, to "The Tonight Show," we were afraid her hooves would slip on the slick floor of the studio, so I arranged for the studio to provide a big wooden dolly, and we rolled her from her trailer to the backstage area. We put a carpet down back-stage with a runner going out to the stage where there was another carpet on camera.

When I took a water buffalo to the "Dinah!" show, the crew neglected to put down a carpet, so I walked out carrying the buffalo, which weighed well over a hundred pounds. When I set it down, its feet started sliding out from under it, so I picked it up again and held it through the whole interview. I was standing there sweating and struggling to maintain my grip, while Dinah went on very calmly, asking lots of questions.

For one "Tonight" appearance, I took on a baby aardvark, Minerva. She had been named after the wife of one of the board members who had made it possible for the Zoo to acquire aardvarks, but the girls in the Chil-dren's Zoo had nicknamed her Krinkles, because a baby aardvark's skin is all crinkly and pink.

She was about a foot or a foot-and-a-half long and one of the most singular-looking animals in existence. An aardvark has ears like a rabbit, a nose like a pig, a body like a kangaroo, a big thick tail, very little hair, and a gray body. In Africa, it's called an "earth pig." I told Johnny that aardvarks are nocturnal and burrow under the ground during the day. "Well, sure!" he said. "If I had a body like that, I'd be nocturnal, too."

But I thought Minerva was beautiful. She had the cutest little nose and big long ears, marvelous claws, and skin as pink as a baby's. She was a beautiful aardvark!

As I often do, I took Minerva back on the show about eight months later, to show how she'd grown. She weighed well over 100 pounds by then. When full-grown, she'd reach about 200 pounds. She wouldn't follow me, and anyway, I didn't want her to slip, so someone handed her to me backstage, and I carried her out and set her down on the stage.

Minerva was the last animal I was showing that night, and when we were done, Johnny said, "Good-bye, it was nice having you on." I squatted down and put my arms around Minerva, but she was so heavy that I couldn't stand up. I was squatting, kind of rocking back and forth, till Johnny finally came over and helped me lift the aardvark and carry it off the stage.

Jack Grant, the prop man for "The Tonight Show," has always been super about finding or improvising anything we need. When I took swans on the show, I wanted to put them in water, rather than hold them, so Jack got a hose and filled a swimming pool and rolled it on camera with the swans floating around in it.

The number of Zoo employees that accompany me to shows varies from two to eight, depending on how many animals go and what size and type they are. I try to take at least one person per animal, preferably a keeper or another person who has worked with the animal, so that the transitions backstage go smoothly. JoAnn Thomas and Boo Shaw often go along with the nursery animals.

We always try to get to the studio a couple of hours before a show is taped. For "Tonight," which is taped at 5:30 P.M., we load the crated animals into a van or carry-all in time to leave the Zoo by 10:30 in the morning. During the trip, we often take such animals as small apes out of their cages and hold them on our laps to feed and tend to them, and it's fun to see the reactions of other people on the highway when they spot one of our Zoo babies through the car window. A stop for lunch somewhere between San Diego and Los Angeles can also be the occasion for giving a llama a rest stop or asking a waitress for a doggy bag so we can take the remains of our salads to an emu.

The first thing we do after we arrive at the studio is get the animals settled in my dressing room, which usually resembles a small and not particularly luxurious hotel room with a couch, a dressing table, and occasionally a bathroom. Not that I mind—if I get a very nice dressing room, I worry that the animals will damage something.

Then I go to Makeup. Most television shows provide people to do makeup, and the bigger shows have hair stylists, too. The hair and makeup departments are set up like beauty salons.

When we took a young ostrich that had been hatched in an incubator to "Tonight," we put a chicken in its cage for companionship during the trip. When we got to the studio, the chicken had pulled the feathers out of the top of the ostrich's head and left it a little bloody. So we took the ostrich to the makeup man, who washed its head and blew it dry with a blow dryer to fluff up the few remaining feathers. Baby ostriches are striped, for camouflage, so the makeup man put a little baby powder on the bird's head, and drew on stripes with an eyebrow pencil. When he got done, that bird looked beautiful.

Shortly before we tape, I get a copy of the script, and I just have time to glance at it to make sure that it's correct. It contains a few facts, questions for the host to ask and my answers, and sometimes stage directions. Here's the entire script for a spot I did on "Tonight" in 1977 with some millipedes:

MILLIPEDES (APPROXIMATELY 8″ LONG)
SHE WILL BRING TWO OUT IN A GLASS BOWL,
PUT ON DESK, AND GIVE ONE TO JOHNNY.

ARE THESE RELATED TO THE CENTIPEDE?
Yes, and there are 8,000 varieties of millipedes. They don't have 1,000 legs, only 240.

WHAT GOOD ARE THEY?
They eat rotting food, they're scavengers. They keep things clean.

HOW DO THEY BREED?
In the usual way and they molt. They are born in three segments. Every time they molt, they add a segment.

ARE THEY POISONOUS?
Only to animals who eat them.

THEY WILL CRAWL ON DESK AND JOAN
WILL EXPLAIN THE STRANGE WALK.

They are from Africa and the largest get to be approximately 1 ft. long.

When you read the scripts, they seem incredibly simplistic (millipedes breed "in the usual way"?) and that's how some television shows run. But they're really intended as a guide for the host. His questions and the stage directions are put on cue cards or a TelePrompTer. If something interesting or entertaining develops with the animals, a host may take things strictly off the cuff and decide to ask questions as they come to mind. But the prepared questions are there on the cards if he or she needs them. Johnny Carson follows scripts less often than other television hosts do.

The animals never follow them.

10

*Live and Wild
Performers*

The night I took the tarantula on "Tonight," I also took a lion. Fred had been raised in the nursery, and I had handled him in public on other occasions, but he hadn't been out of the Zoo for some time, and he'd grown quite large in the interim. When Fred heard the band's music backstage, he became terrified. Music sets animals off more often than anything else in the studio—it's very loud and the backstage area just vibrates with it. Fred became so aggressive that Red and I decided not to take him on because we were afraid he might hurt somebody.

Sometimes I have to handle animals that I haven't had a lot of time to work with, and anyway, there's always a difference between working an animal at the Zoo and working him in a television studio, when he's exposed to conditions that are foreign to him. We never have a real rehearsal, but if I'm showing a trained sequence, I try to run through it in the studio to give the animal a chance to get used to the surroundings.

Understanding what may be frightening or strange to an animal is as important in handling as it is in training. When I take an animal on television, I try to imagine myself as that animal, try to look at my surroundings in the framework in which that animal perceives them.

When viewers watch me holding a cheetah and chatting with a talk show host, they don't notice that I'm constantly alert for conditions that might be frightening, trying to anticipate sudden movements and noises, and watching for any indications—a bristling of hair or quickened breathing—that the animal is becoming alarmed by his surroundings.

There are many physical signs by which I can judge how an animal is feeling or reacting. When Carol is frightened or nervous, as she was before her first "Tonight" appearance, her eyes get so large that you can see the whites around them, her ears stick out, and her tail goes straight out behind her. Sometimes she'll drop her head and trunk, a defensive position in which she's ready to slap out at whatever might frighten her. I can tell when Carol's relaxed, too, just by the expression on her face, and by the fact that she is standing quietly "in her stance"—not jerking around.

Horses, dogs, elephants, and cats all have expressive ears. When they're "on guard," their ears are in an alert position, pointing in the direction of whatever is frightening them. When a horse is mad, he lays his ears back. But like an elephant, he shows fear more in his eyes. A cat twitches its tail when it's mad. The behavior of exotic cats is very similar to the behavior of domestic cats, though they are even more aloof, and they show the same physical signs of fear and anger.

We never sedate animals in order to take them on TV or out in public. An animal might have a bad reaction to a sedative, and it's not worth the risk. Anyway, an animal wouldn't behave normally under sedation. I wouldn't want to show animals that way.

I sometimes take a viewing cage along to shows in case an animal acts up and I'm not sure I can handle him. That way I can show him without taking unnecessary risks. I was glad I had it when I took Jim, the first baby of Dolly the gorilla, to "The Tonight Show." Though he usually took a nap during the day, Jim didn't sleep during the drive up to Los Angeles, so he was very cranky by the time we got to the studio, and he started snapping at people. I was afraid to take him on the show for fear he'd bite Carson. But he was our pride and joy, the first gorilla born at the Wild Animal Park, and we'd been waiting to take him on the show as soon as he was old enough. So instead of taking him onstage in my arms, as I'd planned, I rolled him out in a playpen with the top wired shut. He had a very sullen look on his face, and when Carson knelt down and talked to him and pulled on his blanket through the bars, Jim jerked it right back into the playpen; he wasn't having any part of the whole thing. They went back and forth, getting nose to nose with the bars between them, making faces at each other. It was a wonderful, comical spot, so what might have been a disaster worked out. The audience loved it.

"Tonight" is taped on the day it's aired—it's broadcast on the East Coast just an hour and a half after taping is over—so it's pretty close to doing live television. But even the other talk shows, which are taped from a week to two months in advance, have never edited or reshot my spots. It's strictly one take.

The animals often don't do what I'd like them to do or show themselves to their best advantage. The 500-pound Galápagos tortoise I once took on "The Tonight Show" is an example. Because he was too heavy to pick up, we loaded him into the carry-all with a forklift. We had a plywood box for him that fit in the back, with straight sides so that he couldn't climb them. The first time we'd ever transported a big tortoise, we'd left him loose in the back of the carry-all, and he had tried to crawl over the back of the driver's seat. We'd had to stop and try to push him to the back of the truck.

You can make a tortoise move, and even control its direction to some extent, by tapping on its shell with a stick. But if a tortoise is really obstinate, it's nearly impossible to make it do anything.

Before its appearance on "Tonight," we washed the tortoise's shell and polished it with glycerin to make it shine. When it was time for it to go on, the tortoise walked right out on camera to center stage and stood up and looked at everybody, almost as though it had been cued. We scratched under its head, and Carson looked underneath it, and then we had a whole conversation about it. But when it was time to go off, the tortoise wouldn't budge. Johnny had the stick and was trying to tap it, saying "Stage right," or "Stage left"—whichever way the tortoise was supposed to exit. Finally, we cut to a commercial. The rest of the keepers, who were backstage, came out to help, and together we managed to get the tortoise offstage.

When I did "The Tonight Show" in July 1976, Steve

Martin, who runs a bird of prey show at the Wild Animal Park, also appeared, bringing two talking birds from the show, an African gray parrot and Howard, a myna. The African gray talked on command, and Howard just talked whenever he felt like it, but he was very comical, and usually very talkative. The African gray was on first, and his segment went just great. Then Howard was shown, in his cage, with a boom mike hanging overhead. The idea was that he would just sit and talk, the way he always did during the bird show.

But Howard never said a word. Finally, we excused him, telling Johnny and the audience that he really did talk, but that something must be bothering him. Perhaps the mike hanging over his cage was distracting him.

We took him backstage and waited to see if he might start talking so we could show him after all, and in the meantime, Carson introduced a female vocalist. As she walked out, Howard let out a very loud, very audible wolf whistle. We tried to shut him up, because she was launching into a serious song, and we didn't want to ruin her act, but when she started singing, Howard yelled, "Haw, haw, haw!" Somebody from the crew came running back and said, "Just get that bird out of here. We're picking him up on our sound out front!"

Nonetheless, Howard was invited back for another show, and that time he talked quite a bit. Johnny and he had a little chat and the resulting dialogue was hilarious. Howard spouted phrases and laughter at random, and it ended up sounding as though he were making fun of Carson.

Though I hardly think they make the most memorable spots, people always seem to remember shows in which animals urinate on camera. Actually, there's a good reason why it happens as often as it does. Most animals tend to urinate when they're excited, and a TV studio is a bright, noisy, strange, and threatening environment.

I took an echidna on "Tonight" in 1973. It's a spiny anteater, a primitive, egg-laying mammal covered with short spines, and looks like a porcupine. As a defense mechanism, the echidna can quickly dig a small hole, just deep enough to hide its long snout and feet, leaving only its spiny back exposed, so that it can't be picked up. As I described this, I lifted the echidna up to reveal its soft, vulnerable underbody, and it squirted Johnny and Ed McMahon.

During another appearance just a few months later, I had a water buffalo backstage while I was on showing another animal. I hurried backstage to exchange the first animal for the water buffalo, and as I walked up to the curtain to come back on, I slipped and fell in a puddle it had made. My whole backside was wet when I went back on camera.

As hard as it is to second-guess what an animal is going to do on camera, it's even harder to second-guess what people are going to do. Sometimes I have to work on shows with celebrities who don't appreciate the potential danger presented by the animals.

Once I took a nearly full-grown emu, an ostrichlike bird, to "The Mike Douglas Show." An emu's a powerful bird—an adult emu can break a man's thigh bone with a kick—and I knew at the outset that this emu, Daphne, could be extremely difficult to handle if she became upset or frightened, so I made every attempt to keep her as calm and as much under control as possible. I made sure there was carpet on stage for her, and I tried to handle her in such a way that she wouldn't get excited.

When she was on camera, Daphne was the center of attention, naturally, and suddenly Johnny Mathis, who was also on the show, sat on her, not really putting his weight on her, but straddling her. I've always admired Johnny as a performer, and I know he didn't mean to disturb Daphne; he just wanted to take part in the spot. He didn't realize that he'd put himself in a very unsafe position, and that if Daphne decided to jump up in the air, he would probably find himself flat on his back. Luckily, Mike asked to see the next animal; when I'm on camera it's hard to find a graceful way to say, "Get off the bird."

One of the most popular spots I ever did on "The Tonight Show" was taped in April 1974, with a couple of baby cheetahs. It's been rerun innumerable times—a tight shot of Carson holding the cheetahs up to his face while they licked him and one rested a paw on his cheek.

When I took the cheetahs back again five months later to show how they had grown, they had to be kept in a playpen with a lid wired on top. When Carson walked over to the playpen, they leaped at him, hissing and swatting at him with their paws, and he pretended to be so startled that he jumped back and landed in Ed McMahon's arms. Often they air clips of the two shows back to back on "Tonight Show" anniversaries.

Another spot that became a favorite and has been shown repeatedly was the appearance of a bushdog, Chiquita. Bushdogs are small South American dogs that run in packs. They have very short legs and look almost like tiny bears. Chiquita was extremely friendly, and when Carson picked her up in his arms, she lay on her back and just talked to him, making little murmuring sounds. He sang a song to her, making it up as he went along—"Me and My Bushdog," or something like that. That was in June 1975, and to this day, people say to me, "I remember the time Johnny Carson sang to the bushdog."

I was a bit nervous when I had to take a bearded dragon on the show. It's a lizard that has a fold of skin at its neck that it inflates as a protective mechanism when it's annoyed. The "beard" is spiny, and the effect is one ferocious-looking lizard. I went to Robin Greenlee and Tom Schultz in the Zoo's reptile house to learn how to handle it. Every time the lizard saw a hand coming toward it, it would inflate, open its mouth real wide, and jump up. Tom and Robin kept telling me to just reach in and grab it—but my hand wouldn't move. I knew it couldn't hurt me, but it scared me anyway.

After a while, I got over it. Robin and Tom spent a lot of time helping me, and I enjoy working with reptiles now. I usually make myself do things like that—I just work at them until I feel comfortable. More than anything, I got over my fear of reptiles by just accepting the fact that I was going to be handling them, so I *had* to overcome my fear. With Robin and Tom's help, I learned how to handle them properly so that I had a certain amount of control over them, and that made me feel more comfortable.

I handled a twelve-foot boa constrictor on "The Tonight Show" early in 1976. It was draped over my back, where it hung down and hit the ground, and it hung down another three or four feet in front. It was heavy, and if it had wanted to give me a hard time, it could have, because it was quite strong, but boas are generally pretty calm when they're handled frequently. Still, I told everyone on the set to stay away from it so that no one would get bitten. There's one man at the studio whose job during the show is to pull the curtain back and let people walk through when they are announced. He was fine when he held the curtain back for me to walk out on stage with the snake, but when I tried to walk back off, he became so frightened and backed so far away that he got all wrapped up in the curtain. He was flailing his hands and legs and I started laughing so hard I could barely control myself. I imagine that all that the people in the audience could see was the curtain flying all over the place.

When some clouded leopards that had been hand-raised and were fairly tame were donated to the Zoo, I decided to take them to "The Tonight Show." The smallest members of the leopard family, clouded leopards have an unusual color pattern blending large spots and stripes, and may represent the transition between striped and spotted cats. While I was backstage waiting to go on, the band started playing and the leopards got very excited and scratched Robin Greenlee and veterinarian Jane Meier, who had accompanied them, quite badly. As soon as the music stopped they calmed down, so before I went on, I asked the band to play very, very softly or not at all.

Both the leopards loved to sit on people's heads, and midway through my conversation with Johnny, one of them jumped up on mine. As he hung there with two feet dangling in front of my eyes, I was only too aware of the scratching the cats had just given the people backstage. I knew that if Johnny suddenly had to cut to a commercial and the band started up, I might get all those claws right in the face. So very calmly, right in the middle of our conversation, I got up, walked off camera, and put the leopards back in their cages. Carson went on talking and covered very well.

After I've finished my spot on a show, all the equipment has to be loaded before we can head for home. Everyone's hungry and tired, so we usually stop for a big dinner at some nice restaurant about halfway between L.A. and San Diego. We discuss what went well and what was funny on the show, and what didn't go so well. The pressure lets up and we all have a good time.

After I did a "Tonight" show with a young pygmy chimp—a rare specimen worth at least $50,000—we all wanted to stop and eat. But we didn't dare leave the chimp in the car, for fear it would get cold. It was sound asleep, so we wrapped it up in a blanket in its baby carrier and took it into a restaurant with us. We ordered our meals and waited for our food to come, and just as the waitress headed toward our table with her loaded tray, the chimp woke up and threw off its blanket. The people sitting across from us let out a screech, and we were kicked out of the restaurant instantly. Of course animals aren't allowed in restaurants, but we felt pretty insulted, because we figured that our chimp was cleaner than most children—like all our well-tended nursery babies, he was spotless.

"Mike Douglas" and "Dinah!" are taped relatively early in the day, but by the time we get back to the Zoo after taping a "Tonight" show, it's usually midnight or later, and we hurry to return the animals to their cages in the dark. Sometimes we catch the show on the nursery TV before we leave.

When I do a national talk show, I feel a tremendous amount of pressure—not just because I go on camera, but because it's such a responsibility to take several animals to a Los Angeles television studio and see that they get back to the Zoo safely. I have the most relieved feeling in the world when I've done a decent show, I'm back, and the animals are in their cages.

My family and friends are impressed that I go on these shows, and I enjoy the vicarious thrill they get out of it. But being on television is a hard day's work for me. I enjoy it afterward—I'm thrilled when we're finished and a show has gone really well.

11

The Wild
Animal Park—
A Modern
Noah's Ark

One of the problems inherent in trying to breed wild animals in zoos is that the reproduction of large mammals may be inhibited by lack of space. Confined too closely, the males of a species may fight, or the females may not be able to put necessary distance between themselves and the males. (In some species, males and females remain separate except during breeding.) Two rhinos become extremely rough during their courtship. If you put two Indian rhinos, each worth at least $50,000, in a small enclosure together, you separate them every time it looks like they might injure themselves, because you can't afford to lose such valuable animals. The close proximity of human beings to displays can also hamper reproduction; animals that are elusive or secretive by nature may not breed when exposed to close contact with zoo visitors. As zoos begin to fulfill their modern role as preserves for endangered species, the whole trend in zoo design is moving away from small enclosures of many animals to fewer but larger enclosures that allow for more normal behavior in more natural settings and thus increase the chances of animals reproducing.

Since its founding, the San Diego Zoo has always given high priority to the conservation of animals and paid special attention to endangered animals. In 1972, that interest culminated in the opening of the San Diego Wild Animal Park, an 1,800-acre wildlife preserve dedicated to the conservation of endangered species. There, rare wild animals roam freely over vast expanses, much as they would in their natural habitats. Their environment is controlled only to the extent necessary to provide essential protection and permit observation.

The first such breeding preserve established by a zoo was the London Zoo's Whipsnade. In this country, in addition to the Wild Animal Park, there is the National Zoo's Front Royal, a 4,000-acre preserve in Virginia, and the Bronx Zoo's St. Catherine's Island, which aren't open to the public.

The establishment of such preserves is the logical extension of the changes that zoos, as they assume their conservationist role, have made in the way they acquire, maintain, and display animals. Today, instead of "stamp collecting"—showing one of every species that they can get their hands on—zoos show pairs or groups of animals. To have a single animal of a species is considered almost immoral, and zoos that have one are encouraged to sell it or make it available as a breeding loan to another zoo with animals of the same species.

Zoos have begun to specialize. Instead of showing six types of cats, a zoo may establish one or two large enclosures where there were once several smaller ones and feature perhaps two kinds of cats that flourish in that zoo's climate and physical environment. The San Diego Zoo sometimes sends animals that aren't doing well to another zoo known to do a good job with that species, and other zoos have sent animals to us for the same reason.

The concept of the Wild Animal Park was originated by the Zoo's staff and trustees in 1959, and it was the pet project of Dr. Schroeder when he was the Zoo's director. Before the Park was established, virtually every square inch of the 128 acres in the Zoo had been developed. There was no room to develop large areas for breeding programs involving large mammals, and the only way to get access to that much land was to establish a separate facility.

Concrete plans began to take shape in 1964 when the City of San Diego issued a thirty-year master plan for 11,000 acres it held in the San Pasqual Valley thirty miles north of downtown. Included was a recommendation for a zoological garden to be developed "as an informal exhibition of hoofed animals and certain species of birds in their native habitat." The plan called for the retention of the open character of the valley's environment and its continued function as a natural boundary for the northerly urban growth of the metropolitan area. Under the plan, all the land across from the Park could be leased only for agricultural purposes.

The Park is operated as an integral part of the Zoo, guided by the Board of Trustees of the Zoological Society and the Zoo's director, and it functions under the same type of arrangement with the city that the Zoo does. In order to establish the Park, the citizens of San Diego had to pass by a two-thirds majority a general-obligation bond providing a $6 million lump-sum loan from the city to the Zoological Society, with citizens' backing in case of a deficit. Every other bond proposed that year failed, but the Park bond passed with nearly eighty percent of the vote—the San Diego Zoo has local popular support that most other zoos envy. Ground was broken for the Park in 1969.

While the Park had been in the planning stages long before I went to work for the Zoo, I really became aware of it when the Zoo started moving animals out there and transferring people with whom I worked out there to care for them. Then I got involved in a public-relations capacity. I used to take reporters there and drive them around, describing what the Park would look like when it was finished.

The process of stocking the Park stretched over two years. Once it was certain the Park would be developed, the Zoo began to stockhold as many animals as possible, and then additional animals for the Park began coming to the Zoo for quarantine, so the Zoo was bursting at the seams right before the Park opened.

Before the Park was established, the Zoo held the largest single wild animal collection in the world. But the Park's opening enabled us to ease crowding at the Zoo by decreasing the number of enclosures and the number of both species and specimens there by sending surplus animals out to the Park. As of early 1980, the Zoo inventory was 3,000 specimens of 750 species, and the Park had 3,250 specimens of 260 species.

To enter the Wild Animal Park, visitors walk through the largest flight aviary in the world, a lush tropical jungle where hundreds of exotic birds, most of them from East Africa, soar freely overhead. Immediately, they know they have entered a special world of animals.

In most traditional zoos, animals are shown by species, and closely related species are shown in the same general area. In the Park, animals are grouped in five large geographical ranges. In each, animals from a particular part of the world—North Africa, East Africa, South Africa, the Asian swamps and the Asian highlands—live together. In the East African range, for example, antelopes, giraffes, zebras, and ostriches live together just as they do in the East African wild. While a main objective is to provide an opportunity for endangered and near-extinct species to survive and reproduce, more common animals—giraffes, ostriches, lions, and zebras—are included to maintain representation of species in all areas. The geographical ranges, each as large as or larger than the entire San Diego Zoo, are separated from one another by moats and fences disguised by plants and camouflage paint. So far, roughly 600 acres, one-third of the total land available, have been developed.

All predatory animals—cheetahs, lions, and tigers—are maintained in separate ranges and fed a homogenized formula diet. We've tried to set up as natural a situation as possible and have the animals live as they do in the wild, but it would hardly be practical to allow predators to feed on other animals. It would be impossible, not only economically, but ecologically. We now know how to feed most exotics and keep them alive, but we've only scratched the surface in understanding the delicate balance of wild habitats.

The only way to view most of the Wild Animal Park is from a nonpolluting electric monorail that runs silently on rubber wheels, carrying visitors on a five-mile, fifty-minute tour around the perimeter. Each open-sided, two-car train carries 125 people, and a driver-guide points out animals, discusses their characteristics and habits, and stops whenever there's something especially interesting to look at.

Viewing the Park from the monorail, one is impressed by the Park's beautiful setting—it's surrounded by mountains and natural brush—by its size, and by the space available to the animals. The number and location of the animals, and their activity, varies continually. When the Park opened, we almost had to train people to look for the animals—after years of seeing the Zoo animals always in the same spot in their smaller enclosures, visitors seemed to expect the Park animals to stand posed for them in front of the train. But that's the beauty of the Park—it's never the same twice. A visitor never knows whether he'll spot the rhinos in the water, under the trees, running, or even calving.

Like the Zoo, the Park has an outstanding botanical collection. It's a haven not only for endangered animal species, but for such endangered plant species as aloes, euphorbias, orchids, cycads, and tree ferns; just like animals, plants have become endangered as the result of the destruction of their natural habitats.

When the Park opened, bulldozers had graded off the

land, and it was as barren as a construction project. But landscaping has literally transformed the skyline since then—some of the faster growing trees reached sixty feet in height in the Park's first five years. Today, to borrow Belle Benchley's phrase, it is a man-made jungle. Wherever possible, plants are located in the same range as animals from the same geographical area. Special botanical attractions include a five-acre native California plant canyon, a collection of the world's conifers, and an Australian plants trail.

Sixteen acres of the Park comprise Nairobi Village, which was developed as entertainment for visitors awaiting tour trains. The wooden, thatch-roofed buildings and animal shelters there are designed like century-old African structures, and are landscaped with plants and flowers native to Africa. The Village holds many special displays. Tremendous numbers of ducks, geese, and swans nest in the Waterfowl Lagoon. In the popular Gorilla Grotto, one of the largest gorilla enclosures in existence, fascinating lowland gorillas splash in their swimming pool and climb a huge gymnastic play structure. There's a mile-and-a-quarter-long hiking trail into one end of the Park that affords photographers the opportunity to get pictures of lions, tigers, cheetahs, and rhinos at close range. There are also small mammal displays, a petting "Kraal" (Afrikaans for corral) similar to the paddock in the Children's Zoo, an Animal Care Center similar to the nursery, and gift shops and dining areas.

During the summer, the Park stays open till eleven at night, and with the aid of amber lights, selected because they're least disturbing to the animals, monorail riders can catch a glimpse of the animals' nocturnal world. The animals stand out from their dark surroundings; the zebras, in particular, look iridescent. There's music, and the whole Park takes on a more dramatic, more exotic atmosphere.

The Park has been extremely successful at its intended function. Eighty percent of the animals there that are capable of reproduction have had young, including several animals that we'd never succeeded in breeding at the Zoo. We were never able to raise Indian rhinos at the Zoo, but three have been born at the Park, one of which has survived. In all the years that we showed cheetahs at the Zoo, none was ever born—in fact, there had been only a couple of instances of cheetah births in captivity anywhere— but within two years of the Park's opening, we had our first cheetah breedings.

The Wild Animal Park has emerged as a major animal research center where important work is done to learn more about normal behavior among exotic animals. We compare studies made in the wild with studies made at the Zoo and Park to find out how captive behavior deviates from behavior in the wild, and whether we can make changes within the framework of our organization and the space available to bring about more normal behavior. We can vary such factors as the number of animals, the size of their enclosures, and the degree of human proximity.

Successful breeding of some species apparently depends on the number of animals present. In nature, one species may exist as large herds of females accompanied by a single male. In another species, males may develop territories and females roam from one male's territory to another. If you confine three males and three females of such species in a small zoo enclosure, their breeding may be adversely affected.

During the first four years that the Park was open, the cheetahs were kept in a spacious section completely out of public view and allowed to exist virtually undisturbed. The number of cheetahs living together and the ratio of males to females was varied in order to establish optimum breeding conditions.

Study of the cheetahs, carried out by a student, Rob Herdman, who sat and observed them for several hours every day, indicates that optimum breeding indeed depends on a certain ratio of males and females living together in adequate space. Competition among the males actually brings on estrus in the females—it affects their breeding cycles and their willingness to mate. This kind of research only became possible after the Park was established. By the end of 1978, thirty-six cheetahs had been born there.

Among the other rare or difficult-to-breed animals born at the Park between the time it opened and the end of 1979 are nineteen Przewalski's horses, eight Père David's deer, fifty-two Arabian oryx, three white rhinos, four gorillas, thirty-six addax, ninety-eight scimitar-horned oryx, sixty-five white-tailed gnu, one hundred and eight white-bearded gnu, and thirty-eight Grévy's zebra. The Park's hoofstock collection is the largest in the world.

One reason zoos are intently pursuing the breeding of exotic animals in captivity is practical—with each passing year, the growing scarcity of exotic animals and the growing number of laws restricting their sale and use have increased the cost of animals and decreased their availability. Pygmy chimpanzees, which come from Zaire, have been valued at from $50,000 to $100,000 apiece, though it's probably more accurate to call them priceless, since they are so rare as to be generally unavailable at any price. The San Diego Zoo, which has had pygmy chimps for years, has one of the only reproducing groups in the world. One of the highest prices ever paid for animals was the $120,000 the Toronto Zoo paid for a pair of Indian rhino, and not long ago, the San Diego Zoo paid $60,000 for a pair of bongo, rare antelope from West Africa and Kenya.

But zoos are also going beyond self-interest and joining forces to prevent the destruction of wild species. One of the breeding programs in which the Park has participated is actually bringing the Arabian oryx—a member of the antelope family that once ranged over most of the Arabian Peninsula, the Sinai, Israel, Jordan, and Iraq—back from the very brink of extinction.

Lovely and graceful creatures, the Arabian oryx have been proposed as the source of the unicorn legend; when they're viewed in profile, the long horns that rise almost straight from their brows look like a single horn. Fawn-colored at birth, the oryx turn creamy white as they mature.

Twenty years ago, the Arabian oryx had been all but wiped out by overhunting, and the small number that survived, isolated in Rub'al Khali, Saudi Arabia, were being steadily depleted. In 1962, the Fauna Preservation Society of Britain and the International Union for the Conservation of Nature and Natural Resources of Morges, Switzerland, launched Operation Oryx. Their goal: to capture whatever oryx remained in the wild and place them in a suitable captive environment to propagate, so that they might be saved from extinction.

The expedition they mounted collected two males and

one female, the last animals of their kind ever taken from the wild. A few remaining wild specimens survived briefly, but the Arabian oryx is now thought to be extinct except in captivity.

With the help of the Shikar-Safari Club, a prominent organization of hunter-conservationists in this country, the Arabian oryx were sent to the Phoenix Zoo in Arizona, which is located in a climate like that of their native land. Six additional Arabian oryx already in captivity soon joined the animals in Phoenix—the London Zoo and Sheikh Jabir Abdullah al-Sabah of Kuwait each sent a female, and King Saud of Arabia sent two males and two females from a small private herd. In 1963, the Fauna Preservation Society, the Shikar-Safari Club, the World Wildlife Fund, the Zoological Society of London, the Arizona Zoological Society, and the Zoological Society of San Diego became trustees of the World Herd of Arabian Oryx, established to sponsor the animals and work toward their successful captive reproduction, with the ultimate goal of reintroducing them to the wild.

In 1972, after the original nine animals had produced many offspring, four males and two females were sent to the San Diego Zoo, which placed them in the Wild Animal Park. Eventually a third herd was established at the Gladys Porter Zoo in Brownsville, Texas. (Despite the allure of being able to claim that yours is the only zoo that has a certain kind of animal, any zoo that's committed to conservation no longer wants to have the only major herd of a rare species, because a contagious disease could wipe them all out. The best protection against disaster is to divide groups of endangered animals and locate them at widely separated institutions.) By the fall of 1977, the total population of the World Herd of Arabian Oryx had grown to more than eighty animals; at the Wild Animal Park alone, thirty-four oryx were born by the end of 1978.

In February of that year, the Park sent four male oryx "home" to the new Shaumari Wildlife Reserve, a protected area in Azraq National Park in Jordan. The transfer of the animals was arranged on an experimental basis; when time passed and the oryx were not menaced by hunters, four females—three from the Phoenix Zoo and one from the Wild Animal Park—were sent to join them. This step toward fulfillment of the World Herd's original goal was seen as just the first of several reintroduction programs to take place on the Arabian Peninsula. In April 1978, the Wild Animal Park sent four addax—desert antelope that once roamed much of North America and the Middle East but are also believed to be extinct in the wild—to the Haibar South Wildlife Reserve in the southern tip of Israel.

In 1979, sixteen of the World Herd's oryx were sent to four European zoos. The effort to perpetuate the species was considered so successful that the World Herd organization disbanded, with the participating zoos assuming ownership of the oryx they were maintaining.

As zoos have begun to cooperate for the perpetuation of rare animals, breeding loans, under which one zoo sends animals to another for reproductive purposes, have become popular. One reason is that the sale of an exotic animal—particularly an endangered one—involves tremendous paper work that isn't necessary for a breeding loan, even though the loan may last the rest of an animal's life. It takes three months to a year to get the permits necessary for a commercial transaction—selling or trading animals—but gifts and breeding loans are considered noncommercial.

There are various reasons for zoos to participate in breeding loans. Certain rights remain with the zoo that actually owns the loaned animal, and it may receive some or all of its animal's offspring, depending on the agreement reached by the participating zoos. Sometimes an exchange is involved. Good relations among zoos are perpetuated, and the continued existence of a species may be ensured.

The American Association of Zoological Parks and Aquariums is currently developing a computerized system for cataloging the exotic animals in all zoos in the entire United States, and ultimately, in the world. Using the computer, which records the number, kind, sex, and location of animals, zoos can locate mates for their individual specimens.

When the Wild Animal Park was established, it was hoped that it might become a source of "specimen supply," and indeed, it has become a reserve not only for the San Diego Zoo, but for other zoos that want to acquire some of the animals we are breeding. When we have a surplus of a particular kind of animal, we often sell or give them to other zoos. Sales, trades, gifts, and breeding loans are often arranged through the use of a "surplus list" issued monthly by the AAZPA. The Wild Animal Park, which ships hundreds of animals to other institutions every year, has become an important supplier of such endangered species as Przewalski's horses and white rhinos.

At the Wild Animal Park, we try to breed animals that generally haven't bred in captivity or that we've had little success breeding at the Zoo. We want to breed enough animals of rare and endangered species so that we can protect them from extinction by establishing nucleus herds at zoos around the world. But we need to control the reproduction of some species.

We use birth control for species whose population has grown to a point where we can't house or market their offspring. It's not that we don't *need* the animals—they could be rare or endangered in the wild—but we can only breed animals if there is space for them.

Surplus males are a particular problem. In the wild, the males of many species are solitary, and only prime males breed. Breeding in a zoo requires just one male and a group of females, but the other males, which would naturally establish large territories for themselves, often can't be put together in captivity. Yet zoos haven't the space or money to provide each with a separate enclosure.

Overbreeding is a particular problem with animals like cats, which have a short gestation period. A Siberian tiger, which weighs less than a pound at birth, weighs up to 800 pounds at maturity—and it's mature by the age of two. If we had unlimited litters of 800-pound cats, we wouldn't have anywhere to put them. Captive lions breed like rabbits, and it's almost impossible to find homes for them. On the other hand, it would be difficult to breed too many elephants, which are born singly after a two-year gestation period.

Timed-release hormone capsules, surgically implanted under the skin, are used for birth control in some of the female cats. Surplus males that we don't intend to breed at all, like lions, get vasectomies. Other males that we may ultimately want to breed are kept separate from females.

Of course, when a single male is bred to a group of females, the gene pool is limited. In the case of animals that survive only in captivity, this may ultimately affect the very development of the species. From time to time, zoos ship new animals in from the wild in order to augment the gene pool of some of the species they maintain.

The San Diego Wild Animal Park is an attempt to provide a protected area as an alternative to total destruction of exotic animals in the wild. It's a more natural environment than that represented by the traditional zoo, but it's not a natural environment. The natural range of one of the large cats at the Park might be much greater than the twenty-acre enclosure in which it is confined. The only way to provide a true natural environment for wild animals is to preserve the natural environment as it is, and that has already become almost impossible. In the future, if there is any "wild," it may well be a wild managed by men. In the face of that reality, the San Diego Wild Animal Park is a model for the zoo of the future.

12

London Holiday—
Zoo Style

In 1972, the activity surrounding the opening of the Wild Animal Park led, indirectly, to my first trip abroad. It was to be the first of many trips in this country and overseas that have acquainted me with the wide range of animal-oriented organizations in existence today.

When the Wild Animal Park opened in May, the weather was so hot that the monorail track expanded and the trains kept breaking down. There weren't many completed displays in the Village area yet, so Red and I were told to take Carol up to the Park and entertain people.

Dr. Schroeder, who had seen elephants bathe at the River Kwai in Burma, decided he wanted to have elephant bathing at the Park. Basically it meant my going swimming with Carol three times a day in an area dubbed the Elephant Wash in Nairobi Village. Carol used to go completely underwater, putting the tip of her trunk up and breathing through it like a snorkel, and I'd go right under with her—she was always careful not to step on me or hurt me. I'd scrub her with a wood-handled brush, and when I was all done, she'd throw dirt all over herself, just like powder.

We followed the bathing with a brief obedience training demonstration in which Carol lay down, picked things up, and followed other basic commands. Some days she would paint, and other times we'd just show how she had learned to swing her paintbrush.

During the first months of the year, I put in the equivalent of three months of overtime promoting the Park and working there with Red and Carol. In September, as compensation, the Zoo sent me to England on a ten-day study trip to visit zoos and parks and observe animal training techniques. Arrangements were made for me to stay with the Chipperfields, a family of animal dealers who first developed drive-through parks in England and went on to establish others in Scotland, throughout Europe, and in the United States. They were good friends of Dr. Schroeder, and I had once had lunch with the head of the family, Jimmy Chipperfield, and his daughter Mary when they visited the Zoo.

I was very excited to be going to Europe for the first time. Mary Chipperfield and her husband, Roger Cawley, picked me up at the London airport, and during the days that followed, they drove me through their wildlife parks. I also visited the London Zoo and Whipsnade, the London Zoo's equivalent of our Wild Animal Park. The first open-space breeding farm ever established by a zoo, Whipsnade is similar to the Park in that it has very large enclosures, but visitors walk through it or drive around the perimeter.

The vegetation at Whipsnade was incredibly lush and green, but to me, accustomed as I was to the dry climate of southern California, all of England seemed extraordinarily lush and green.

I spent one afternoon shopping in Harrods, London's enormous, world-famous department store. When I heard someone calling "Joan! Joan!" I didn't pay any attention, because I figured nobody in England knew me, but the next thing I knew, the San Diego Zoo's curator of birds, K. C. Lint, grabbed me by the arm. He was in England for a waterfowl convention, and I went along with his group to the private reserve of Chris Marler, a wealthy Englishman who raises racehorses, exotic waterfowl, and Scottish Highland cattle. He had a beautiful collection of geese, cranes, and flamingos, many caged but some in large open enclosures. Marler had done a fabulous job with his collection. Some private individuals who have the necessary money and expertise do a far better job with exotics than many zoos.

Woburn Abbey, which I also visited, is another excellent private preserve. It is owned by the Duke of Bedford, who, like many members of the British upper class, has had to open his estate to the public in order to pay the staggering English taxes. Both the house and Woburn Wild Kingdom, which was developed by the Chipperfields and displays lions, giraffes, white rhinos, cheetahs, and baboons, are open to visitors.

Woburn Abbey has been instrumental in preserving Père David's deer, which have owed their continued existence to preservation in captivity longer than perhaps any other exotic species. While they once lived in the swamplands of northeast and east-central China, they have been extinct in the wild for 3,000 years. For most of that time, a herd survived in the large Imperial Hunting Park just south of Peking.

The first Père David's deer exhibited in Europe were received in London in August 1869. In 1894, after obtaining specimens from continental European zoos, the Duke of Bedford—grandfather of the current duke—began breeding Père David's deer at Woburn Abbey.

During China's Boxer Rebellion, which culminated in 1900, the walls of the Imperial Hunting Park were broken down and the deer there were scattered or killed, some slaughtered for venison by foreign troops. Some were sent to Paris and Berlin, and others were taken within the Peking city walls. By 1912, only two specimens remained in China, and both were dead by 1921.

The species's survival depended on Woburn Abbey, half a world away. Today Woburn Abbey has 300 to 400 Père David's deer, which are kept in a separate area not open to the public. A number of herds descended from Woburn Abbey stock are now in zoos around the world, including the San Diego Wild Animal Park.

While Woburn Abbey has been an animal preserve at least since the turn of the century, many other English estates have established animal attractions in recent years, coincident with their opening to the public. The Chipperfield family supplied animals to many estate owners and holds an interest in several of these parks.

While I was in England, I also toured the Bristol Zoo, one of the most beautiful zoos I have ever seen. Located on a seaport, it is beautifully landscaped with flowers and immaculately maintained. It's a relatively small city zoo, but a truly outstanding one. It has a very select group of animals, including such rare species as okapis and white tigers, all prime specimens and all extremely well cared for. The Bristol Zoo has had unusual success in breeding not only okapis and white tigers, but marmosets, gorillas, and orangutans.

Geoffrey Greed, the zoo's director, showed me around and asked if I would like to see their baby orangutan. I assumed that he was going to get it from a nursery, since most of our orangs at the Zoo have been hand-raised, but to my amazement, he walked out a 150-pound female that was carrying her baby and holding on to Geoffrey's hand. I had never seen grown orangs handled in a zoo, especially not females with offspring, which can be quite dangerous. But keepers in many European zoos maintain closer contact with their animals than we do in San Diego, and in Bristol, that closeness was facilitated by the zoo's limited number of animals.

Mary Chipperfield was just a little older than I, pretty and petite, with dark blond hair usually pulled back in a ponytail. She was a real animal nut, and her dad, whose family ran the Chipperfield Circus, had bought her her own traveling circus. Its nucleus was the Circus Enis Togni, which he had brought from Italy to England and embellished with additional acts.

About fifty people worked in the circus, and they all lived in trailers. They'd set their tent up in a town, unload their menagerie of trained animals, and perform for two or three days, then tear it all down, load up all the animals, and set off for the next town. I traveled with the circus for about a week, living in Mary's big trailer and sleeping in a bed not much larger than the Great Dane that shared it with me. Whenever the circus arrived in a new town,

they'd parade through the main street with the elephants
to announce their performances, and I paraded with them
and helped the elephant trainer.

The circus workers lived a very vigorous life-style. An
incredible amount of time went into practicing. Though
I found it almost impossible to drag myself out of bed in
the dark, cold English mornings, the crew would get up
before dawn to start working the animals, going through
the entire show. After a break for tea, they would go out
and clean the area and give the matinee performance,
and then they would get the animals all set again and do
the evening performance. Each show included all kinds
of animal acts and ran about an hour and a half. The work
day ended about ten or eleven at night.

Mary worked the horses, putting them through the
showy riderless routine called "liberty" and doing "high
school" riding, which blends the subtle maneuvers of
formal dressage riding with flashier movements like bow-
ing and marching. She also worked the tigers and worked
an elephant with a Great Dane.

Mary's husband, Roger, ran Lions of Longleat, the
drive-through park, opened in 1966, which started the
trend of establishing safari parks on British estates. Begun
with an exhibition of lions, the park grew to include a
school of hippos, a large chimpanzee family, a Monkey
Jungle with 200 baboons, and a 100-acre East African
Game Park area that holds the largest herd of giraffes
outside of Africa, together with zebras, antelopes, ostriches, and other large animals and birds.

Roger and Mary had a big home, Longleat, nearby,
where they kept a lot of animals, including quite a few
cheetahs. Roger stayed at home with their little boy and

little girl and brought them to visit the circus every few days.

Mary ran the circus because that was what she loved to do, and I thought it was great. I didn't end up wishing I was running a tent circus in England—much to my mother's relief—but I admired Mary, and I envied her because she could work so many animals and live and travel with them. Working for the Zoo, my contact with animals has always been far more restricted than hers.

Until I went to England, the only animal operation with which I was familiar was the San Diego Zoo. Since then, I've visited a tremendous variety of institutions, some geared toward education and some toward entertainment. No zoo—not even the San Diego Zoo—has everything. But the more I've traveled, the more I appreciate what the San Diego Zoo does have—not just in terms of tangible goods, but in terms of climate, popular support, and reputation.

13

Cody and Rufus

After I got back from England, Red and I began to divide our time between the Zoo and the Park. I was still making all kinds of public appearances, and I began to collect and maintain a small group of animals that were not of use for breeding programs or display in the main zoo so that I could always count on having animals available that were trained or at least accustomed to my handling them. I wanted to feed and care for and work with them as they grew, so that they would accept me when they were adults. If you intend to handle exotic animals beyond the baby stage, you have to work with them every day.

Early in the summer of 1973, Red and I drove to Tucson to pick up two baby animals—a cougar, which we named Cody, and a North American timber wolf, Rufus. Cody was given to us by the Arizona Sonora Desert Museum because they had a surplus of males, and it was through them that we learned of Rufus, one of a litter that belonged to a Tucson couple who owned wolves privately. They hadn't intended to breed them, because they didn't have homes for the offspring, but the wolves had managed to overcome whatever obstacles had been placed between them and reproduction.

The wolf and cougar are beautiful and fascinating native American predators. Cougars once ranged over the entire continental United States, but they were hunted for sport and were driven out of much of their range by ranchers who feared they would prey on cattle. They now exist in this country only in sparsely populated areas of the Southwest and the Rockies. When I acquired Cody, so many cougars had been killed off that there was a moratorium on killing them while attempts were made to determine how many cougars survived. The timber wolf also had a large North American range at one time, but by 1973, it was even more rare than the cougar.

Cody and Rufus fit my need for show animals in several ways. The reduction in their species as the result of competition with man for space and food illustrated the plight of wild creatures. And certainly the price was right—they were free because they were "surplus" animals, not needed for breeding. Size was also a factor; Cody and Rufus would be handleable adults if raised properly. To be quite honest about it, a full-grown lion or tiger just isn't a safe animal to work with. You can find a lot of people who say they are, but if a 400-pound cat gets frightened, there's no way you can physically control it. It's not easy to control a 200-pound cougar, either, but it's a much more reasonable proposition.

Rufus was eight days old when we got her and about

the size of a puppy of the same age. Cody the cougar—
also called a puma, mountain lion, or panther—was about
two weeks old. Like all baby cougars, he had spots all over
him; they're camouflage for babies in the wild until they're
between nine months and a year old. Rufus was very
timid, but Cody was a feisty little guy and put up a fight
over everything.

The first night, Red took the wolf puppy home and I
took the cougar. By then, I was living in an apartment of
my own in the suburbs. Cody was hungry, but he didn't
associate a bottle with food, so it was a fight to get him to
eat, and he kept crying and growling and carrying on. He
made such a racket, I was afraid he might get me kicked
out of my apartment, so I took him into bed with me and
tried to feed him and keep him quiet, but he screamed
most of the night.

Rufus and Cody were to be maintained at the Zoo especially for our use, and Red and I raised them ourselves.
We wanted them to think of us as their source of food and
attention. By the time such animals are three months old,
they don't transfer readily from one handler to another.

Elephants and apes react to their surroundings with
some intelligence, but "lower" animals tend to react more
from instinct, and to handle them you need to override
their natural behavior patterns somewhat and get them to
accept things they wouldn't normally accept. They need
to grow up thinking that having you around is the usual
order of things. You also want to establish, before the animal is large enough to become a threat to you, that you're
dominant, and that you won't allow certain types of
behavior.

Red and I used to take turns driving in at night to feed
Rufus and Cody until they were off bottles, and often I

would stay right at the Zoo till I was through with the night feedings and then go home. I like the Zoo at night, though it's a little eerie at times. It's very dark, and in the absence of the Zoo's thousands of daily visitors, animal noises pierce the silent air. Red and I practically lived with Rufus and Cody, and we had to put in three months of work on an everyday, around-the-clock basis, before we could really do anything but mother them. But that's what makes good, handleable adult animals.

In nature, wolf packs pose the greatest threat to cougars, and cougars, in turn, prey on wolves. But Rufus and Cody lived right next to each other, with adjoining runs, so they developed an unusual tolerance toward one another. They played together as babies, but in time they just got too rough and we had to separate them because we were afraid they would hurt each other.

Rufus grew to be a beautiful adult animal. Her coat was gray, with a silvery sheen, and she had a long bushy tail, big ears, and big canine teeth. Full-grown, she weighed about 125 pounds.

She was extraordinarily affectionate with Red and me. When I approached her cage, she'd get really excited, whining and making a funny low growling noise. When I went in, she'd jump on me like a dog greeting its master and grab my arm gently with her teeth; wolves in the same pack greet by grabbing each other's noses. If I sat down, she'd crawl up in my lap and lick my face.

But our use of her was limited to things we could show people at a distance, from a stage, because she became very nervous when she was approached by strangers. The hair would go up on her back, a fierce look would come into her eyes, and she'd growl, sometimes even bare her teeth. She occasionally snapped at people, but I always had her under control on a leash.

Her behavior was typical of wolves. Like elephants, wolves are social animals, and in the wild, where they live in packs of up to thirty animals, they have a very tight social structure. If hand-raised, they may become very affectionate with the people that care for them, but are still wary of strangers—it's probably a manifestation of their pack instinct. We took Rufus on a TV show when she was five months old, but we weren't able to handle her in a TV studio after that. She just got to be too un-trustworthy in strange circumstances. It wasn't something that could be overcome—it was her nature.

Cougars, by nature, are independent and solitary. In the wild, they stake out individual territories of several square miles and live as solitary hunters except during the breed-ing season, when they travel in pairs. In captivity, they are relatively indifferent to their human keepers. When I would go into Cody's cage, he would acknowledge my presence—he'd make a "rowh, rowh" sound as a greeting and come over and rub against my leg, but where Rufus might have been saying, "I'm so glad to see you; I want to sit on your lap and be with you the whole time you're here," Cody's message was, "Oh you're here. I'll rub up against your leg and then I'll go sit in the corner." He didn't want the closeness that Rufus did. Interestingly, wolves are related to domestic dogs—they're the largest wild members of the dog family—while cougars are re-lated to domestic cats, and the same characteristics are seen in their domestic counterparts: dogs tend to be de-voted and affectionate, while cats are more aloof.

Cody was buff-colored, with a white belly and dark

142

gray ears, and he had a beautiful face with big, dark eyes and long whiskers. Like most cats, he embodied a blend of grace and strength that was enhanced by his aloof and regal air.

Cody traveled very well and was pretty good around people, so when he got older, I took him to cocktail parties, luncheons, and dinners around San Diego. He had a cage that fit in the back of my truck, and he'd always jump up into it eagerly. Like most wild animals, however, Cody had a short attention span—when he went somewhere, he'd sit and be very, very good for about half an hour, but when he'd had enough, that was that. He'd want to leave, and if he couldn't leave, he'd be irritable.

It's a problem when I'm handling animals and people want to tie me down to a schedule. They say, "Could Joan bring that cougar to lunch for an hour?" But I can't say to a cougar, "Okay, you've got to work an hour today." If he gets fed up, he's fed up. I can try to pacify him, move him around, keep his mind occupied, and discipline him, but after a point, I've just got to put him away. More than once, I realized I had one hell of a lot of cat on the other end of that leash, and that if Cody wanted to be ornery and knew his own strength, I'd be hard put to control him.

Once, at a cocktail party at the San Diego Press Club, he grew tired and cranky and grabbed the dress of a woman who was petting him. I was afraid he might bite her, because when he got hold of something, he was often extremely possessive about it. He'd growl if I tried to take it, and I pretty much had to leave him alone until he lost interest in whatever he'd taken. This time, to my relief, he let go quite readily.

When Cody was nearly two years old, he and I sat in the Children's Zoo every day, all day, for a weekend, so that people could take pictures of us and talk to me. We handed out photographs of us that were autographed with my signature and Cody's paw print. It was pretty rough trying to keep Cody quiet for a whole day, and he was beginning to grow irritable when a photographer arrived to get some shots for a local newspaper. His motor-driven camera kept going "Zing, zing, zing," as he circled us, getting closer and closer. I told him to keep his distance, but he got just a little bit too close, and Cody reached out and grabbed his leg and scared him half to death. The photographer called me later that afternoon to ask if there were any shots he should get, and I suggested a tetanus shot, but he wasn't really hurt.

Cody bit me once. I was walking him down a hill at the Zoo, and he was moving fast because he was eager to get back to his cage. Scrambling to keep up, I stepped on his tail and—it was so fast—the next thing I knew he had sunk his teeth into my leg, all the way to the bone. He let go as soon as I got off his tail—it was just his instinctive reaction to being hurt. He didn't stop to think, "Hey, she didn't mean it."

Because of his relative tractability, we used Cody several times for promotional and advertising photographs. The Zoo sometimes makes animals available for advertising photography in exchange for shooting fees or credits, but clients are carefully screened. The Zoo doesn't do ads for liquor or for controversial products that might not reflect well on the Zoological Society, nor do we train animals to do specific behaviors for ads.

Whenever people use Zoo animals in photographs, I tell them in advance, "You have to understand that you're going to work around the animal; the animal won't work around you." When we used Cody for ads, I had the agency people get the camera, the model, and the product all ready before I even brought him out, because I knew I couldn't keep him interested in what was going on for more than a few minutes.

A lot of the animals that become TV "stars" or work regularly in commercials and advertising are chosen because they are exceptionally good-natured. Unlike Carol and Robella, two highly intelligent and social animals, Cody and Rufus really had to be appreciated at a more fundamental level, for their wildness and beauty. Raising them made me realize that when one becomes involved with such a wild creature, one is responsible for it for the rest of its life. As a consequence of the daily concerns of caring for and worrying about Cody and Rufus, I became tremendously attached to them—in some ways, I suppose, I became more dependent on them than they were on me. We were lucky to find each other, really, for it might have been difficult to find homes for "surplus" animals like Cody and Rufus, had I not been able to "use" them to communicate with people about conservation problems.

14

The Elephant Show

About a year after the Wild Animal Park opened, a more experienced animal trainer, Don McLennan, was hired to work with Red and me. A short, soft-spoken guy in his fifties, Don was a free-lancer who had started in the business as a trick rider and roper in a Wild West show and gone on to work with circuses. He was best known in the animal-training world for his work on the movie *Doctor Dolittle*, for which he trained dogs, horses, chimps, and birds, as well as the giraffe on which Rex Harrison rode. Red and I both looked forward to learning from someone with his background.

After Carol and Sumithi had left the Children's Zoo, two younger elephants, Jean and Joan, had taken their places. John Muth had named Jean after Jean Hoch, the head attendant in the Children's Zoo, and Joan after me, partly because I'm such an elephant nut. Animals are named after Zoo employees with some frequency, but it's still an honor—in this case, it had been announced to the press and pictures had been taken—and I had been very flattered. When they were old enough, Jean and Joan had been moved to the Park, and Red and I had begun using them as well as Carol for the elephant bathing. Soon after Don's arrival, he and Red and I decided to teach the elephants more advanced and entertaining behaviors and to create a real elephant show.

The concept we developed then has been the basis of every animal show I've done since. The show was to be entertaining, but as a production of the Zoo and Wild Animal Park, it also had to be educational. We wanted our audiences to walk away with a new understanding of and appreciation for elephants. We always referred to the elephants' activities in the show as behaviors, rather than tricks, and while we did think up a few zany stunts for them to do, most of the things they did—including sitting, lying down, standing on their hind legs, and kneeling— are behaviors that have been observed in wild elephants when they are feeding, breeding, or playing.

The narration that accompanied the show told something of the history and geographical distribution of elephants and described some of their mental and physical characteristics. The many behaviors they performed with their trunks illustrated the strength and versatility of that unique organ. Other behaviors demonstrated that elephants, despite their bulk, have remarkable balance and agility. We explained that obedience training not only helped us control these huge animals, who were potentially dangerous, but that training the elephants was important for their physical and mental health in captivity.

The Elephant Show

The training and exercise kept them from getting bored and neurotic. We did the show—three times a day during the summer and two in the winter—in an amphitheater at the Park that consisted of a ring and bleachers.

When Don came to the Park, Red and I had just gotten some tubs and had started trying to teach the elephants to sit up on them. With him there to guide us, we succeeded in teaching them that and many other behaviors. We built a cart and a howdah—a structure in which Asian work elephants carry things on their backs—and Carol would load logs on the howdah while one of the other elephants loaded logs in a cart. We also got into more "cute" tricks—we taught the elephants to wave bye-bye with their trunks at the end of the show—and we undertook to teach them some more dramatic physical behaviors, like walking on their hind legs.

All three of us worked all the elephants, and each animal had a different personality. Jeannie was the tough one when it came to training. She was an extremely athletic elephant—she could turn quickly and stand on her hind legs—and she was very quick to learn. But she didn't like people much; she just didn't want to be bothered with them. Her idea of working was to run through everything and get it over with so she could go eat and be left alone. She often did ornery things, like tripping us on purpose when we were running next to her, or, when she was loading logs in a cart, picking up a log, whipping it around fast, and hitting one of us in the head with it. If you knew Jeannie, you knew it wasn't an accident. But she wasn't vicious, just irritating.

Joan was more of a klutz—she was a real blocky, squared-off elephant, and she didn't have Jean's natural balance and control—but she was more lovable. She was sort of slow and methodical, and like Carol, she was easy-going about training and took it all in stride. That kind of elephant tends to be a steadier performer, the kind of animal you can take anywhere and let people get close to. Jeannie's type—nervous, high-strung, super-intelligent, very fit, and ready to respond—must be watched all the time. They get bored and tend to accept less from people. But some trainers prefer them because they're fast, flashy performers.

Red and Don and I continually tried to think of different routines to add to the elephant show, not just for the elephants' sake or for the sake of publicity, but for our own sakes as well—as a challenge. It was fun to try to think of something we could teach an elephant to do that an elephant had never done before. When we were asked to haul the elephants from the Park to the Zoo to do a special show at a picnic for Zoo members in the fall of 1973, we racked our brains. What could we do for the members that would be different from what they could see at the Park every day?

There was supposed to be a sea lion show at the picnic after the elephant show and we hit on the idea of trying to work Carol and a sea lion together. The question was whether we could get them comfortable enough with one another to work in such proximity.

The first day we brought them together, the sea lion came gliding out of the water and barked and scared poor Carol half out of her skin. The sea lion was decidedly unconcerned about Carol, but Carol was totally unprepared for a creature like the sea lion, with its peculiar way of waddling along the ground. But we began to work them at a distance from one another, and as they became accustomed to each other's presence, we gradually brought

them closer together. By the night of the picnic, we'd per-
fected a whole routine. Carol hit a ball into the pool and
the sea lion retrieved it and gave it back to her. Then
Carol picked up water with her trunk and gave the sea
lion a bath. Finally, the sea lion picked up an apple and
carried it to Carol, who took it from the sea lion and ate it.

The same night, we paired Carol with Jeannie for a
bowling routine. First Carol rolled a bowling ball toward
some pins with her trunk, taking two tries, just like in a
regular bowling game. Then Jeannie took her turn, kicking the ball toward the pins. After her second try, she ran
down and kicked over the pins left standing—a poor elephant sport if you ever saw one.

During performances, Red and Don would stay on the
sidelines, handling props and elephants, while I worked
in the ring. At certain points, when we had two elephants
doing different routines, as when one loaded logs on the
cart and another loaded the howdah, Red would join me
and work one of them.

Don wanted me to do the shows because it was a novelty
and an attraction to see a woman working with wild animals. He wasn't one of those jealous trainers—and there
are many—who only let their assistants shovel elephant
manure. He didn't really care about being in the spotlight,
and I benefited from his attitude.

Occasionally I felt guilty, though. From the time Red
and I had started working together, his job had been to
back me up in my role as goodwill ambassador, but I had
often felt funny about getting all the attention, because
he always worked as hard as I did. When Red and I put
on shows together, we both worked the elephants, but Don
tended to push me into the spotlight and minimize Red's
role.

Because of his circus background, Don put a lot of emphasis on styling, as they do in circuses. He wanted me to be aware of my own position while I was working the animals, and to strike a graceful and dramatic pose—pointing my toe, gesturing with my arm, and so on. Till Don came along, my style had been no style. I was concerned about my grooming and my outfit, but in the ring I had always concentrated on the animal's performance, not on whether I was smiling or pointing my toes or looking feminine. Don made me much more aware of my own presence in the show ring, and persuaded me that it's a valid concern: the audience looks at the people as well as the animals in a show. Today I make sure that any people I train are aware of their stance in front of an audience, although I don't think that all the flash that you see in circuses is necessary or appropriate in a zoo.

Before long, we worked Cody, Rufus, and Don's leopard Appaloosa horse into our daily shows. After we showed the elephant behaviors, I'd bring out the horse, Jimmy, and put him through a liberty routine. A liberty horse, usually seen in circuses, performs a variety of movements—a waltz, a rear, a bow, a march, a change of direction, and a figure-eight—without a rider, in response to a voice command or whip cue. Don had trained a lot of liberty horses, and he taught me how it's done.

In the wild, animals tend to do what is easiest. They aren't free spirits; their existence is shaped by such pressures as available food, nearby human populations, and other animals of their own or other species. In the face of these pressures, they generally follow the path of least resistance. An animal trainer can't always physically dominate a powerful animal like a horse or a cougar or an elephant, so he has to find a way to make the thing he wants an animal to do the path of least resistance, the easiest way out. The training of a liberty horse is a good example.

During training, you work the horse on a "lunge line" attached to his halter or to a "lunging caveson," a special halter with a ring on the noseband. The line controls the horse's speed and position, and until he performs consistently, you never take it off. You work the horse until he's so conditioned that by the time you take the line off, the trained behavior has become habit.

You also use a "lunging whip," which is about five feet long and has a five-foot lash, not to hit the horse, but to guide him. The whip becomes an extension of your arm, and he responds to its movement.

To teach the horse to move forward in a circle, you stand behind him and drive him forward with the whip while controlling his front end with the lunge line, starting with a very small circle. If you want the horse to slow down, you pull him back with the rope, and if you want him to speed up, you get behind him and drive him a little more. At the same time you use vocal cues like "Whoa," or "Get up."

For many maneuvers you use your body position to position the horse. To "whip break" him—teach him to come when you call—you stand in front of him and flick him on the flank with the whip, walking backward until he comes to you. Every time he turns his hind quarters to you, you flick him on the flank to keep him moving forward. Historically, whip-breaking was used to catch horses in a field or pasture, since it's far easier than chasing them.

152

With similar techniques, you can teach the horse to change direction and perform a figure-eight—two successive changes of direction. To teach him to rear, you tap his front legs until he begins to lift them off the ground, reward him, and continue to work with him to increase height, balance, and duration. If you tell a whip-broken horse to rear, then call him to you, he will begin to step forward, and once he develops the necessary strength and coordination, he'll walk on his hind legs.

Teaching the horse to bow is very simple: you pull his leg up and hold it. The other leg gets tired and the horse—to make himself more comfortable—drops his shoulder to relieve the strain caused by the position in which you've put him. When he does that, you reward him. One horse may take ten minutes to bow the first time, and another may stand there for an hour. But if you're patient, the horse will bow. And immediately there is a reward—food, praise, or just letting the horse go on with whatever he was doing before. Food is usually used in the early stages of training, but may be eliminated later.

Though the lunge line is about twenty feet long, you begin training with the horse only about five feet away from you. As he learns the cues, you move him out gradually until you can work him at the end of the line—and ultimately, without any line at all. If you take the line off too early in training, the horse learns that he can do something other than what you want, and you have to put the line back on until he realizes he might as well perform correctly. From time to time, you have to vary the order of your commands, so the horse doesn't become "ring-wise" and begin to work by itself because it knows its routine. When that happens, you're no longer in control.

❉   ❉   ❉

After Jimmy performed, I'd bring on Rufus and Cody. By then, Rufus was trained to a leash and would sit and lie down on command, but she had too short an attention span and was too nervous to be trained more than that, so the narrator just talked about her. We trained Cody to sit up on a pedestal, roll over, and jump from one pedestal to another—the kind of things you see cats do in circuses.

Cougars aren't normally working cats; by disposition they're not as easily trained or as reliable as lions and tigers. Actually, you see the same few types of animals— lions, tigers, elephants, and European brown bears— worked again and again in circuses and shows, because they are more amenable to training than other species. Cody didn't always like to work, and we had to be pretty firm with him. We used food rewards to some extent, but he was too independent to work well for food.

Like liberty training a horse, training a cat involves positioning a large and powerful animal without direct physical contact. Training a cat also requires a whip, with which you make a popping noise or flick him lightly—in either case, he'll want to get away from it. The first thing we taught Cody was to stay on a tub or pedestal unless we asked him to do something else. When he got off his pedestal, we'd crack the whip and it didn't take long for him to learn that his "safe" spot was on the pedestal. This gave us control.

To teach Cody to sit up, we'd tap one of his feet until he picked it up, then tap the other foot. The first time we touched him, he'd leave his pedestal, but we'd drive him back to it and try again. As soon as he sat up, we'd reward him and leave him alone for perhaps five minutes—long enough for him to understand that he had accomplished the appropriate behavior. Then we'd ask him to sit up again, going through the training again and again until he would sit up on command.

To teach him to jump from one pedestal to another, we put a leash on him and used the whip to drive him off one tub and onto another. If he jumped off the second tub, we'd put him back up on it, again repeating the training until he understood that he was to jump to the next pedestal and hold that position.

To train Cody to come to us, we'd tease him with the whip, tapping him on the shoulder or hindquarters or head until he began to move toward us. Then we'd back off and draw him forward again. When he came, we'd reinforce the behavior with food he especially liked or with praise and stroking.

We used the leash to teach Cody to lie down, just pulling him into position, and once he learned to do that, we taught him to roll over. We'd begin by tapping him at the side of his head with the whip till he moved away from it—the start of the roll. When his head was almost over, we'd tap his back, causing him to reach around, and then we'd tap his feet and he'd roll all the way over. Once he knew the behavior, we'd use the whip as a cue, not even touching him with it—we'd just position it toward his head and he would roll over.

Working a cat is a great challenge. Certain trainers love to work cats and think animals like elephants are dull or have no pizzazz, while other trainers love elephants and don't like cats. A lot of it has to do with the trainer's personality and the approach he likes to take. Some people like to come on tough and have an animal fight them, and some like an animal that just goes along with them. Some trainers, especially those in circuses, like lots of show, with whips and guns and chairs. I was fond of Cody and I liked the challenge of working him, but my own preference is to work an animal that enjoys working and seems to look forward to seeing me. It's for that reason that I especially like elephants, the great apes, and other animals with a social nature.

In time, we backed off from training and working Cody because of the need to use a whip and assert a forceful, dominant personality. Carrying a whip alienates a certain number of people who don't believe in its use, and it wasn't practical to open each show with a discussion of how and why we discipline animals. Finally we decided it wasn't worth it, even though it was a treat to see a cougar work.

I didn't find the use of the whip offensive at all. Someone who says, "She's carrying a whip—she's cruel," is mistaken. A well-used whip is a tool and a signal. To use a whip badly is cruel. Various devices that are used to control animals—whips, spurs, bull hooks, choke chains, and bits—have all been associated with cruelty by some people, but they are only as cruel as the people who use them.

Actually, a trainer who's rough or cruel usually doesn't get anywhere with an animal, because the animal becomes too frightened to understand or think about what the trainer is asking him to do. Over the long run, the animal may become terrified of people. That's what happened to Cha Cha, a six- or seven-year-old elephant that was donated to the Zoo about the time we started doing the elephant shows.

A previous owner had hit Cha Cha again and again with

a bull hook, hard enough to puncture her skin hundreds of times. She had large abscesses all over her body because the wounds hadn't been cared for and turned into boils. Some mistreated animals become extremely aggressive, but Cha Cha was just terribly afraid of people, and the slightest touch with a bull hook made her take off running. Most animals will allow themselves to be restrained to some extent, but Cha Cha was terrified of any kind of contact. She was too frightened for us to be able to communicate with her at all, and the bull hook, which is normally used to control an elephant, had the opposite effect on her because it had been used improperly.

Red and I worked with Cha Cha briefly at the Zoo. Then she was moved to the Park with all the rest of us, and though she wasn't part of the elephant show, we continued to work with her when we had extra time. We trained her as we would any other elephant, but we had to go at it much, much more slowly. After we'd worked with her awhile, she'd come up and see us along with the other elephants when we approached—touch us and sniff us and explore us—but the minute we made any move toward her, she'd take off. We had to gain her confidence and get her to understand that training wasn't all pain.

It's much easier to work with an animal that's never been handled than with one that's been mistreated; it took a very long time to undo the harm that someone else had done. But Cha Cha did respond to proper handling. An elephant trainer who began working at the Park a couple of years after Red and I continued to work with Cha Cha, and today she works every day giving rides to Park visitors, something that requires a well-disciplined animal with a good, steady temperament. She's a dependable elephant, fond of people, and easily approached. The real problem was never with Cha Cha, but with her first handler.

One afternoon in October of 1973, Joan became sick very suddenly. The other elephants in the enclosure sensed immediately that something was wrong—elephants are inclined to stay close to one another and touch one another and are always aware of each other's whereabouts—and they became very distressed. They began to make low grumbling sounds and gathered around Joan where she lay on the ground and started touching her with their trunks and pushing her with their feet. Elephants in the wild have been seen to do the same thing, to lift or support a wounded or ill member of their herd. On this day, however, the concern and aid of her own kind were of no help to Joan, and she died within hours.

Though a postmortem examination was done—as it is done on every animal that dies at the Zoo—the cause of Joan's death was never determined. I was terribly sad. Ironically, I'd been especially happy that the Zoo had named Joan after me because elephants live for such a long time. I thought that for the next sixty years there'd be an elephant at the Zoo named Joan. That's one of the things I like about Carol—provided nothing goes wrong, she'll be around for a long time. When you become very attached to an animal with a shorter life span, you always face the pain of losing it. I often think that when I'm older, if I'm no longer involved with the Zoo, it will be neat to go back and visit Carol.

When Jean and Joan left the Children's Zoo, they had been succeeded by another baby, Scout. The Zoo had always acquired elephants in pairs, because of their social nature, but after Jean and Joan, the Zoo could only afford to buy one at a time. Prices had gone up dramatically because elephants had become a protected species and shipping costs had risen. When Carol was acquired in 1968, she cost $3,200. Today, an elephant costs over $20,000.

Don and Red and I began to work with Scout while she was still in the Children's Zoo. She always made me think of a big dog, because she used to tag around after me, and like a sheep dog, she had bangs that came all the way down to her eyes. She was kind of awkward, like any baby elephant, and her bangs, all bleached out at the ends, gave her a very comical aspect. Like all the other elephants, Scout learned to sit on a tub, and every time she did it, she turned her tail off to one side and put it up in the air or wrapped it around her hind end so that she wouldn't sit on it.

When Scout was about three years old, another elephant was acquired for the Children's Zoo, and Scout joined us at the Park and began to work in the daily elephant show. Because she was so young, she was kept separate from the other elephants in a bull pen up on a hill.

At the beginning of the elephant show, we used to "tail up" the elephants—one elephant following and holding on to the tail of the one in front of it, just like you see in circuses. It keeps the elephants in a group and serves as a kind of control—when an elephant's got hold of the tail of the elephant in front of her, she's thinking about that. If you have a "bad" elephant, you can put her between two good elephants to steady her.

When we added Scout to the group, we started tailing her up with the bigger elephants. They'd take off around the ring, and she'd go scrambling after them with her ears whipping around and her feet flying, hanging on to the next elephant's tail for dear life. Sometimes it would fly out of her trunk and she'd run like mad to catch up. She was a very diligent elephant and took her training quite seriously, and she knew she wasn't supposed to drop that tail.

We had trained Carol to play the drums, hitting the bass with her tail and the snares and cymbals with her trunk, and then doing a little shake, a dance. Don and Red and I decided to put together an entire elephant band, with Jean on harmonica and Scout on piano.

To teach Jean to play the harmonica, we held the tip of her trunk wrapped around it, and whenever she made a noise, we rewarded her. Actually, we were teaching her to blow on command, and again, it was a natural behavior—the same means an elephant uses to blow dust and water on its back. For Scout, Don built a wooden piano that looked just like a real one and set a keyboard into it, because a regular piano was more than we could afford. We put the piano in the training area, and if, in her exploration of this new object, Scout touched the keyboard, we rewarded her. Then we'd wait for her to touch it again and we would reward her again. Sometimes we'd press her trunk against the keyboard to make a sound, and then feed her. We kept at it till Scout associated that behavior with reward.

Whenever Scout played piano, she'd cross her hind legs and stand with a nonchalant air, as if to say, "This is no big deal." I often thought she liked certain combinations of tones, and at times, it sounded like she was playing a real tune as she went up and down the keyboard. Eventually, because she was smaller and easier to transport than Carol was, we started taking Scout to television shows, and in April of 1974, she appeared on "Tonight," playing the piano.

One morning a few months later, when I went up the hill to feed Scout and bring her down for the show, I found her very, very sick—she wouldn't eat and had very bad diarrhea. I was panic-stricken, because there's not much you can do for an elephant when it gets sick, and it was just a few months since I'd seen Joan get sick and die in a single afternoon. I called for medical help, and the minutes crawled until the vets got there. But they couldn't figure out what was wrong with her, and I knew that made things worse.

The vets did everything they could for Scout and left, and I had to go back down and do the elephant show without her. I was depressed and worried. I hoped the vets might figure out what was wrong with Scout and pull her out of it, but I couldn't shake the knowledge that she probably wasn't going to make it. When I was right in the middle of the show, I saw the veterinary truck going back up the hill, and I knew that Scout had died.

I don't think I've ever cried as much as I cried then. It was far worse for me than Joan's death, because I'd been much more closely involved with Scout, working with her day after day. I felt like I'd lost a member of my family.

I was in tears most of the day, but still I had to go out again and try to present a lively and entertaining show. The whole sequence was thrown off—I'd be going through a routine and I'd turn around to look for Scout, forgetting that she wasn't there, and be jarred all over again. The elephants were confused too.

For weeks, whenever the elephants tailed up and I went

through the line, I'd get to the end and start to reach for Scout. Then I'd realize all over again that she was dead, and everything would seem empty.

When you work with exotics, there's always a certain percentage of fatalities, though the mortality rate at the Zoo drops continually as the staff learns more and more about proper housing, diets, and medical treatment. When I first started working for the Zoo, every animal had a name and a personality, and I became very attached to each one. But I soon learned that I can't take all the Zoo's animals home with me every night. I can't stop them from being transferred to another department or even out of the Zoo. When the Zoo sells an animal that I've worked with since it was a tiny baby, it's painful, but I've learned to accept it. And I can't stop them from dying. I had to learn from the beginning to accept the death of animals, especially young animals, because many that are in the nursery are there for medical attention. I get shook when an animal dies, but I know I can't allow it to overcome me. I still get attached to animals, but my feelings are more guarded than they were when I began. I don't think I'm hard, just more realistic.

15

House Pets

When I was a kid, there was a bowling alley right below our house at the bottom of a hill. One summer all the kids in the neighborhood signed up for bowling lessons and kids' bowling leagues, and my mother signed up my sister and me. I used to go to the bowling alley with everybody else, but I never bowled, because I wanted to save the money for horseback riding. When my mother found out after a few weeks that I wasn't bowling, she was furious and threatened to stop giving me the money.

For as long as I can remember, I wanted a horse. I continually begged my parents to let me go riding, and every now and then I'd get to go out on a trail ride, or my dad, who knew just a little about horses, would take me to the mountains to ride.

Finally, when I was about thirteen, my parents, worn

down by my determination, began to send me to riding school. I used to look forward to it all week long. I would do anything—clean the house, scrub the floors, do other chores—so that when Saturday rolled around I'd be free to go riding.

Every Friday night, I'd iron my riding clothes, polish my boots, and curl my hair—the only time I ever cared about what I looked like was when I was going to the stable. I took lessons all through junior high school and high school, eventually going into private lessons and beginning to ride some of the American saddlebred gaited horses.

Southern California is horse-owning country—San Diego County has the second highest concentration of horses of any county in the nation. After I graduated from high school and began working at the Zoo, I started showing horses. I had to wait until I had a job to support my interest, because my parents, though they had come to accept riding for recreation, thought it was frivolous to spend money to show horses. To them it was a whole life-style that was beyond our means.

My first showing experience was in three-gaited plea-sure classes, competing on horses belonging to the owner of the stable where I took lessons. I used to pay the entry fees and the cost of hauling horses to shows, and I had to save every penny I could to buy the right clothes. In the beginning, I must have looked pretty funny, because I used to borrow clothes or buy used outfits. I can remember when I couldn't afford one pair of britches, and my sad-dle suit was a hand-me-down that I had remade to fit me.

Gaited horses have to have special high platform shoes, and because of the set that holds their tails up in the air, they have to have special stalls with tailboards to keep them from rubbing against the wall. They require almost constant training to keep their "action" up; they have to be jogged every single day. Board for a gaited horse runs $200 a month and up, and shoes run $40 to $50 a month. Before long, even though I was doing fairly well in competition, I realized that it was beyond my means to ever be able to really compete with gaited horses, and I knew I was never going to be able to own a saddlebred myself.

So I started taking jumping lessons, and then I began showing hunters—jumping horses—over fences. I also learned dressage, a style of riding in which the coordination between horse and rider is so developed that the horse can be cued to move in any direction at any speed without the cues being apparent to the audience. With every passing year, I became more and more determined to own a horse of my own.

My dream finally came true in 1973. I was going with a guy named Don then, and we sometimes drove up to a horse ranch outside of San Diego to look at horses. During one visit, I fell in love with a little half-Arabian foal. He was brand-new and still with his dam, a chestnut foal with legs like stilts, white socks on his right front and left hind legs, and a little white blaze on his nose. His father was an Arabian and his mother, a quarter horse, and he had a "typey" Arab head—in horse jargon, that means his head had a typical Arab configuration, with wide, prominent eyes and a small muzzle. The ranch owner let him and the mare out into the arena and he ran around behind his mother with his tail straight up in the air like a flag. He was so cute, I just wanted to pick him up and hug him.

While I was hanging over the fence, adoring the foal, Don disappeared for a while with the ranch owner, Dick Cessna, but I didn't think much about it—I figured they'd gone to look at some of the other horses. Then, when we were driving home, Don said, "Happy birthday. I'm getting you that little foal." Don was in the truck equipment business, and Dick had a tractor that needed painting, so Don had worked out a trade.

I was overjoyed. The only hitch was that I had to wait until the foal was old enough to be weaned before I could have him. It seemed to take forever, but whenever I could, I'd drive to the ranch and visit him.

Purebred horses can be registered if both the mare and the stud are registered animals. The sole exception is the Arabian horse registry book, in which half-Arabs can be registered, in a separate registry, if either the mare or stud was registered. Because of their versatility and fine qualities—their refined look, beautiful carriage, arched neck, beautiful head, stamina, intelligence, and speed—Arabs are often bred with other kinds of horses. My foal's registered name was Raj by Rhamoun; his father was Monty by Rhamoun; and his grandfather, a stud well-known around San Diego, was Rhamoun. From the very start, though, I called him Finally.

When Finally was five months old, he was weaned and shipped to Don's house, where there was space for him, because I was still living in an apartment. From the day he arrived, I began to spend almost every minute that I wasn't at the Park working with him. In the beginning he was very susceptible to colds and other infections, and once, when he was sick, I drove to Don's house every morning and every night to give him shots. I doubt that there's ever been a horse that was handled more; I practically slept in the corral with him. Because he was a baby, I couldn't ride him, but I'd walk with him for miles. I'd even put his halter and lead on him and take him with me when I went to the grocery store. He was like an obedience-trained dog. And it's left its mark on his adult personality; he's very oriented to people and affection. To this day, when I drive in at night, he'll whinny and greet me, while other horses wouldn't pay much attention— unless it was feeding time, in which case they might knicker a little.

For a long time I had thought I'd like to shoe horses for a career, and after I got Finally, I began going to horse-shoeing school two nights a week and all day Saturdays. I learned how to use a forge, how to make a shoe by hand from a piece of flat bar stock, how to control horses during shoeing, and how to use corrective shoeing on animals with leg problems. I found out how taxing shoeing horses is physically. It's a real art, and it takes a great deal of time to learn how to do it properly and quickly.

When Finally was about a year old, Don sold his house, so I started boarding Finally at a horse ranch in Bonita, another San Diego suburb. I wouldn't be able to start riding him until he was almost three, but I did begin to train him to do the liberty routines I'd learned from Don McLennan.

As he got older, Finally began to get white hairs, even entire white spots. It looked like he might have some Appaloosa in him, and the bright coloration of an Appaloosa would be very undesirable in a half-Arabian, which is prized for its Arab traits. But by the time Finally was two, his coat was roan—kind of salt-and-pepper, like the hair of a person who's going gray. Then he began "dappling out," and the next thing I knew he was a beautiful rose gray. Gray, a predominant color in Arab lines, has always been my favorite color for a horse, and it's not unusual for an Arabian that's born a bay or a chestnut or black to turn gray as he matures. When a chestnut colt, like Finally, turns gray, the sprinkling of chestnut hairs gives the gray coat a warm, rosy cast—rose gray.

When Finally was salt and pepper, he wasn't a terribly attractive horse, but when he started "rosing out," he really started getting beautiful. People would just rave about his color. Finally grew up to be a much finer horse than anyone could have guessed when he was a spindly-legged foal being traded for a paint job.

Not long after Don McLennan came to work at the Park, I went to his ranch with him to see his horses. I rode one of them, a gray Thoroughbred named Eagle that Don had purchased not long before from a racetrack training facility. Eagle was seven years old and had raced for five years, and Don had bought him for high school training, a kind of circus riding that is similar to dressage but is not performed to the same rigid standard. It takes five or six years to develop a dressage horse—it's almost like developing a ballet style—but by relaxing the standards somewhat, you can teach a horse similar movements in a much shorter time, and to the untrained eye the effect is very similar.

Don had found that he didn't have time to train Eagle as he'd planned, and was thinking of selling him. Because of his conformation, I suggested he would make a good junior hunter. In horse shows, jumping horses are shown in either hunter or jumper classes. Hunters are judged on their conformation, manners, style, and way of going— their smoothness. They come into fences on stride and take them one after another without stopping. Jumpers are judged solely on their ability to clear jumps. A jumper can trot or walk or canter or gallop to the jump and can be the ugliest horse in the world—if he can make it over the fences, he can be a champion.

Eagle was an athletic animal and had the smoothness to compete as a hunter, but he was a little too small to be a top contender in open classes, those in which adult riders compete. A perfect candidate for open championship is between 16 and 17 hands high—a big horse. (Horses are measured from the ground to the shoulder, and a hand is four inches, so a horse 17 hands high is 68 inches—5 feet 8 inches—at the shoulder.) Eagle was 15.3, a little under the ideal.

I'm 5′ 10″, and when I got on Eagle, he looked shorter than he really was; a small rider, by the same token, would make him look bigger. In a junior class, where the riders are all under eighteen Eagle would not be faulted for his size. From a sales point of view, Don would do best to show Eagle to someone who wanted a horse for his child to show.

By the end of the afternoon, Don and I had agreed that I'd move Eagle out to the ranch where Finally was boarded and start training and conditioning him. If I could find somebody to buy him, Don would pay me a percentage. It was a great arrangement for me. As much as I loved Finally, I still had a year to wait before I could start riding him, and I was getting impatient. If I took Eagle, I'd be able to ride and work him while I looked for a buyer.

As soon as Eagle got to the ranch, I put him on a really good diet and groomed him and got his feet done and started working him over fences. He was a dark steel gray—that was one of the most appealing things about him—and when he was all cleaned up, he was a nice-look-ing animal. After about six weeks, I began showing him to people. I put a pretty good price on him, and the second couple that came out to look at him said, "We'll take him."

170

At first I was excited that I'd done so well. But then I started thinking about giving up Eagle, and I realized I couldn't bear to part with him. So instead of making a little money, as I'd planned, I raided my savings account and bought him from Don myself. From that point on, I was committed to a high overhead for animals. It cost me close to $200 a month just to feed and board Finally and Eagle and keep them in shoes. But it was like a dream for me. All my life I'd been riding other people's horses, and now I had a horse of my own to ride and show.

Eagle was always hot-tempered. When I was training him, if he didn't understand something or got tired or irritated, he'd just pin his ears back and blow a fuse, bucking and kicking. My sister Janet put one of her friends on him one day and he dumped her and she broke her arm.

What balances Eagle's hot temper and small size is that he is one of the most athletic horses I've ever dealt with. He can jump five-foot fences and turn on a dime. Some bigger, lankier horses can take a fence and look pretty, but after riding Eagle, riding them is like driving a Mack truck.

About the time I got Eagle, I began to grow concerned about Max, a Britanny spaniel that my parents had owned for years and years. He was growing old and debilitated, and I was concerned about the pain my parents would face when he finally passed away. We had owned springer spaniels in the past, and my parents had always been very fond of them, so I began looking for a springer puppy to give them for Christmas. I went to a breeder to look, and as usual, I ended up falling in love with half the animals in the place, especially Brave, the five-year-old father of the puppy I got for my parents. About six months after I visited, the woman who bred the dogs called me to say that she and her husband, who was in the service, had to move. "I know how much you liked the dogs," she said. "Would you be interested in taking Brave?" Of course I was; I was dying to have him. I'd never had a dog of my very own. I couldn't keep him in my apartment, but I was so excited, I told the woman that if she'd hold Brave for about a week, I'd find a new place to live.

Now that I had Eagle, I was spending more time than ever at the horse ranch where he and Finally were boarded. The ranch owner had five houses there that he rented out, so I arranged to move into one of them. It overlooked the ranch, which consisted of a large riding ring that could be lit in the evening, a long row of barns, a "hot walker" or electric horse walker, and a bull pen, a small ring for lunging. Just beyond the ranch was the river, and a big dam could be seen further down the valley; it was a beautiful setting. I'd always lived in strictly residential areas, but I'd dreamed of living in the country since childhood. It was a big thing for me to be able to live in a house again, and at last I was able to live close to horses—my horses.

When I went to pick up Brave, I worried that he might pine for his old owners, but he accepted my new home as his from the very beginning. We went everywhere together. I usually took him to work with me, and on my lunch hour, we'd run through the Park. In the evenings, he'd go with me to lectures, and he slept in bed with me every night.

Brave was the kind of dog that mothered everything; he got along with every kind of animal and wouldn't hurt anything. When one of the ranch owner's dogs got into the cage of a rabbit I had and injured it, I patched it up as well as I could and put it in the bathtub, and Brave sat in the bathroom all night with his head hanging over the tub, keeping watch.

For a while, I kept one of the Zoo's African gray parrots at home to use for my lectures. African grays are the best talkers among birds. One day I walked into the house and found Brave running around in frantic confusion while the bird, sitting in its cage, called again and again—as it had heard me do so often—"Come here, Brave! Come here, Brave!"

At last my life was beginning to assume the shape I'd always planned for it. I was making a living at the best job I could possibly imagine, and now I was doing well enough at it to have the horses I'd wanted for so long. On many nights after I'd worked late at the Park or been kept out late by a TV show or lecture, I'd go back to the ranch and ride late at night under the lights—sometimes it was midnight or one o'clock—with Brave loping round and round behind the horse. To some, it might have seemed a lonely life, but I was happy and at peace, doing the things I'd always loved to do.

If I stopped working for the Zoo tomorrow, I would still have a life filled with animals, because they have always been my hobby, as well as my job. I acquired one of my all-time favorite pets, a baby fox squirrel, right after I started working at the Zoo, when I was still living with my family. Fox squirrels run rampant at the Zoo, where they have a habit of climbing into the peanut-vending machines and eating all the peanuts, so that customers get an empty bag in exchange for their quarter. During a big spring storm a nest blew out of a tree, and a visitor found two tiny babies, only a few inches long, and brought them to the Children's Zoo. They needed to be hand-raised on bottles, so another girl and I each took one home. When she got a little older, I named mine Miles, because she covered so much territory.

In the beginning, I used a little doll bottle to feed Miles her formula. She needed to be fed every few hours, but Mom and Dad both worked, so my twin sister, Linda, and I, who were both going to San Diego State, started taking her to school with us. We used to carry her in an open satchel with a blanket inside. Miles would sleep during classes, and nobody even knew we had her in there. Between classes, she'd wake up and we'd walk around campus, taking turns letting her ride on our shoulders.

It was our freshman year, and Linda and I were in the same English class. One day during English, Miles woke up and started getting rambunctious. The instructor broke off right in the middle of his lecture and turned to stare at my purse, which was jumping up and down on my desk. I tried to look as though I didn't notice it, but Linda, who was sitting just a few seats away, started to crack up.

All of a sudden Miles jumped out of the bag and started tearing around the room, with Linda and me in hot pursuit. Several girls started screaming, while most of the guys were laughing and trying to help us catch Miles. We finally cornered her and put her back in the purse and covered her up.

After that, Miles couldn't go to school anymore, but she was getting older and didn't have to be fed so often, anyway. She was a funny little creature. She liked me and my mother and my sisters and all our girl friends, but she disliked men. If Linda or I had a boyfriend over who wanted to see the squirrel, she'd attack him. Every time my dad got near her, she'd jump at him, and she even bit him a couple of times.

Linda and I got in trouble more than once because Miles got out of her cage and chewed things up. She disconnected the phone a couple of times and severed a lamp cord, and my mother really hit the ceiling when she bit off all the piping that ran around the edge of the couch and the whole thing had to be recovered.

When she matured, we moved Miles into a wonderful big cage in a tree outside the house. It had a little "bedroom" partitioned off by a blanket, and she liked to sit in the bedroom and peek out, enjoying her privacy. We used to buy her the best nuts we could find, and we kept feeding her more and more of them till we discovered she had stockpiled pounds of nuts under her blanket. That squirrel really had it made.

One day Linda and I had Miles out, playing with her, when we realized we were late for school. Mom said she'd put the squirrel back in her cage, so we took off. But Miles decided to play a game, refusing to get back in her cage, and finally my mother got so exasperated, she just gave up. When Linda and I came home, Miles was nowhere to be found. She had run up a pine tree and disappeared. For two days, we mourned our lost squirrel, while my mother felt guilty and miserable. We were all sitting glumly at dinner the second night when Miles's little face appeared, looking in at the window. For two days, while we were sure she was gone forever, she'd been living on the patio. We put her back in her cage, and from that day on, she seemed perfectly content. She lived to be almost ten years old, an exceedingly long life for a squirrel, and, I like to think, a very pleasant one.

*　*　*

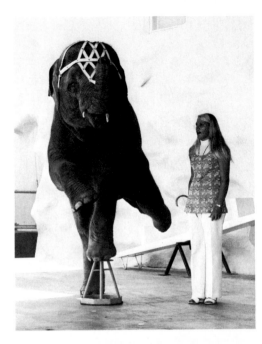

Despite their size, elephants are agile and have excellent balance. In 1972, in shows in the Zoo's amphitheater, Carol demonstrated these traits by sitting up, standing on her front legs, walking and turning on a narrow balance beam, and balancing on one foot on a pedestal.

Left: Carol also learned how to load logs. For centuries, elephants have been used as work animals, moving and loading logs, in the teak forests of Asia.

Below: By 1973, Carol was more than seven feet tall and weighed two tons. She was—and still is—my first love at the Zoo.

During the early days of the Wild Animal Park, Red and I used to bathe Carol to entertain visitors.

Above: Red and I raised Rufus, a North American timber wolf, from the time she was two weeks old, and she's still appearing in shows at the Zoo today.

Below: We acquired Cody the cougar, also an infant, at the same time we got Rufus, and they were raised in adjacent pens.

Above: Scout's shaggy bangs gave her a comical air.

Below: Don McLennan, at left, had a fantastic imagination for thinking up routines for the elephants. Scout on piano, Jean on harmonica, and Carol on drums made up our elephant band at the Wild Animal Park. Red's in the center.

It took considerable training to get Carol to accept as strange an animal as this sea lion; the first time she set eyes on it, she tried to turn tail and run.

Getting three elephants— here Carol, Jean, and Scout—to sit up simultaneously is a real training achievement.

Scout was intelligent, but she wasn't always accommodating. When we wanted her to put her front feet up on the back of a pickup to make a picture for the company that donated the truck to the Zoo, she wouldn't have any part of it. Finally we used Carol, who would do virtually anything we asked.

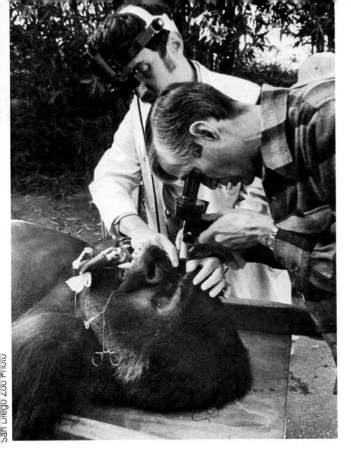

Left: The San Diego Zoo has one of the largest veterinary staffs of any zoo in the world. Here, Trib, the Wild Animal Park's massive lowland gorilla, undergoes a checkup.

Below: A second floor observation area allows students and visiting professionals to witness surgical procedures in the operating room of the Zoo's new hospital, which opened in 1978. In the hospital's first surgery, a female cougar received a contraceptive hormone implant.

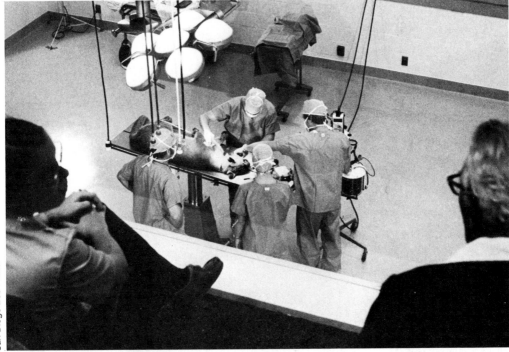

Above: When First Lady Betty Ford visited the Zoo in 1975, I took her into the enclosure to meet Connie, the Children's Zoo's baby elephant.

Below: Jimmy Carter visited the Zoo during the last weeks of his 1976 presidential campaign. Chuck Bieler, director of the San Diego Zoo, is at center.

I was pleased and embarrassed at the same time when the Zoo decided my new animal show warranted billboards around San Diego.

Above: For the new show, I had just a few weeks to teach newcomer Kathy Marmack to handle Carol, by then a very large elephant, but Kathy had the determination to succeed. Getting Frisky, a guanaco; Anastasia, a red-tailed hawk; and Carol to all cooperate for this photograph was in itself quite an accomplishment.

Left: When Carol lifted me in a "trunk mount," I was easily ten feet off the ground. The one time I fell, Carol was far more upset than I.

Above: When I traveled to Africa, I finally had the opportunity to see these peaceful giants in their wild environment. This herd of elephants passed just outside our lodge in the Mara Serena preserve.

Below: Of course, wild elephants aren't always peaceful. When I took this shot, Jumbo, the mascot elephant of the Mara Serena Hotel, had just taken a refreshing drink from the lodge water tank after demolishing two cars in the parking lot in a search for food.

Joan Embery

Above: Rhinoceroses are poached for their horn, which, when ground up, is prized as an aphrodisiac in the Orient. Within a week after five Southern white rhinos were introduced to the Meru Game Park in Kenya, two were slaughtered. The remaining animals are now followed at all times by armed guards.

Below: When we visited a Masai "manyatta," or village, in Kenya, we had the opportunity to observe many of the Masai's tribal customs.

Bob and Geneva Stone

San Diego Zoo Photo/Ron Garrison

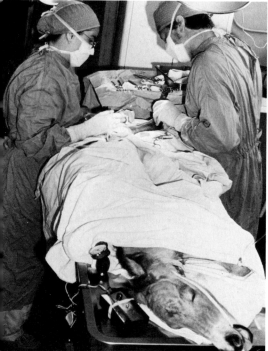

San Diego Zoo Photos/Donald Meier, Phil Robinson, D.V.M.

Above: Przewalski's horses are believed to be extinct in the wild in their native Mongolia. By early 1979, fourteen had been bred at the Wild Animal Park. Bogdo, shown here, is one of two foals that suffered broken legs shortly after birth, probably as a result of being stepped on by another member of the herd.

When Bosaga, a Przewalski's filly, suffered a broken leg within twenty-four hours of birth, doctors Phil Robinson, director of veterinary services, and Jane Meier resorted to an advanced technique of human medicine— bone-plating—to stabilize the fracture. A lightweight Fiberglas cast eased the period of healing.

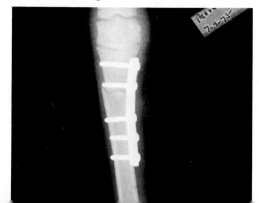

m a single species, the Przewalski's horse, man has used selective breeding to develop
ses for a great variety of domestic uses. Large draft horses, like this Clydesdale, Melodie,
e developed for use in battle in medieval times. Miniature horses, like Atlas, twenty-nine
es high at the shoulder when full grown, were bred as novelty pets.

975, after wanting a horse for as long as I
uld remember, I was given a little half-Arabian
, which I named Finally. When he got older,
ained Finally to do "liberty," a discipline
ally seen in circuses, in which the horse
forms "at liberty"—without a rider.

Eagle, my gray Thoroughbred, exemplifies the
athletic qualities of the horse. In the horse show
at the Wild Animal Park he performed a hunter-
jumper routine, clearing four-foot fences.

Kenya's massive baobab trees take hundreds of years to grow.

Though formidable looking, the Kikuyu dancers who performed for us at the Lodge in Kenya were extremely friendly.

A kill: A side of animal life one never sees in a zoo. A lion devours a water buffalo.

Denise Demong

At home on the ranch, Petunia the pig knows that when Finally gets a bath, it means a great mud hole for her.

Chuck Barber

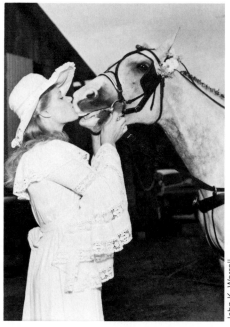

Above: Finally gets a kiss for making it to the church on time.

Left: Duane and I are never happier than when we're in jeans and cowboy clothes and working on the ranch. We used this picture, in color, on the front of our wedding invitations.

I get attached to all my pets. I have a tendency to take on animals whenever they're offered or whenever it's possible for me to figure out a way to keep them, and once I've had them even a short time, I don't want to give them up. Since I could afford to feed animals, I've found myself with a growing collection that takes most of my salary to maintain. As my income has increased, so has the number of animals I have and my food bill.

Right now, in addition to Finally, Eagle, and Brave, I have a Great Dane, a pig, three ponies, two pygmy goats, a parrot, a parakeet, and an ever-growing number of cats. Though I spend my professional life handling exotic animals, most of my pets are domestics, and I speak out at every opportunity against people keeping exotics as pets.

After they've seen me on television, the first thing some people want to do is run out and get an exotic animal for a pet. But within a year's time, ninety-nine percent of those who do will want to get rid of them.

People who want exotic pets generally have no idea what they're getting into. People who think they'd like to own a chimpanzee have usually only seen baby chimps. They don't think about what they'll do when that baby grows into a 150-pound adult. When people adopt a cute little lion cub, they don't anticipate the day it will start tearing things up, getting nasty, and eating them out of house and home. The animal will simply grow to be the wild animal that it is, but most people are under the impression that if they treat it as a pet, that won't happen.

Exotic animals can be hard to handle and generally take more time to care for than domestics, and it's not easy to turn their care over to other people. They require specialized diets, and most veterinarians can't or won't deal with them. Just as important, many exotics are potentially dangerous and present tremendous liabilities to owners. A private owner could be wiped out by a lawsuit if a pet that is termed exotic hurt somebody. In most areas, it is illegal to keep exotic pets, but most people don't know that when they buy one, and there are plenty of dealers who will sell people a chimp for five hundred to a thousand dollars or a cougar for three of four hundred dollars, knowing full well that the animal will eventually be confiscated.

When people express interest in acquiring wild pets, I suggest they confer with their local animal regulation department, their veterinarian, and their local zoo on the management of the animals they're interested in. In most cases, if someone looks into the problems of keeping an exotic, he'll decide against it.

As long as people buy young wild animals for pets, traders will supply them, and in the process, they kill off twice as many animals as they sell. For every little spider monkey that is brought into this country and makes it into someone's home, there are two others that don't survive—because they are killed in a bungled capture attempt or get sick or won't eat, or just because of the stress of being captured and transported. Most of the exotic pets that do survive finally end up in a zoo for the rest of their lives, because that's the only place that can keep them.

The San Diego Zoo gets lots of calls from people who don't know what to do with their exotic pets and want to give them to the Zoo. But the Zoo hasn't the space or the budget to be able to take on all of them. The animals most frequently offered are monkeys—spider monkeys, squirrel monkeys, capuchin monkeys—and lions, which breed so readily in captivity that even zoos have a hard time unloading them. But the Zoo tries to maintain a collection that is representative of the animal world, and it can't accommodate 200 spider monkeys.

It's unusual for people to donate rare or valuable animals, though a woman once called wanting to give the Zoo her chimpanzee, and it turned out to be a pygmy chimp. Unlike common chimps, pygmy chimps have hair on their faces, but for some reason, the woman had shaved her pet, so we didn't realize at first what we had.

The privately owned animals that are given to the Zoo are often in poor health when we receive them, frequently as a consequence of poor nutrition, which can lead to obesity, deficiency diseases, even death. The Zoo once received a pair of chimpanzees, Bonnie and Clyde, that had bad cases of rickets because they hadn't been fed properly. Their eyes bulged out, and their bones were almost like rubber. They had to crawl everywhere, because they couldn't walk or even stand up. But after several months on a diet very high in calcium and vitamins, they were able to move normally once again.

Such mistreatment of exotic pets is usually the result of ignorance on the part of owners, and ignorance can also extend to handling. Once the Zoo received a cougar that had been confiscated by the Animal Regulation Department. The man who owned him had taken him to affairs all around San Diego commercially, drugging him to keep him tranquil. The cougar wouldn't accept handling, because he'd never been handled by anyone but his owner, and he had been declawed and defanged, so he couldn't live with other cougars. Finally he was sent to a rehabilitation project in another state.

To be fair, there are a few private individuals in this country—just as there were in England—who do an excellent job of keeping exotic animals. Some people who have private collections, particularly those who specialize in a single species, do as well as zoos in their areas. They can give full attention to their specialty, one thing that's hard to do in a zoo, where so many animals are maintained.

Although I'm critical of most people who want to keep exotics as pets, I was once one of those people. I've had exotics at home, and I've had the problems that go along with them. I've learned what a tremendous burden they are, and my experiences have shaped my opinions.

16

A Vet in the House

A few months after I went to live on the horse ranch, Jane Meier, a senior vet student at Purdue University in Indiana, came to work at the Zoo under a special study program. Jane shared my love for horses, and we became friends when I invited her out to the ranch to ride with me.

When it was time for Jane to leave the Zoo, she told me that she had applied to return for an internship, and I said that if she was accepted, she would be welcome to stay with me at the ranch. She was and she did, and shortly after the internship ended, Jane went to work as a full-time staff veterinarian. So instead of being a summer guest, she ended up living with me for three years.

Spending time with Jane reawakened my interest in veterinary medicine. Every night, we would discuss what had happened at the veterinary clinic that day, which animals had been worked on, and what had been done to them. Sometimes I went along with her to the Zoo when she needed help with an animal, and when a dog on the ranch was hit by a car, I assisted her, handing her tools and sponges, in a spleen surgery.

The field of zoological medicine—veterinary treatment of exotic animals—is just now coming of age. Ten years ago, only ten zoos in the United States and Canada had resident veterinarians, and in 1978, there were thirty-eight resident veterinarians, at thirty zoos. Many small zoos just use consulting veterinary clinics.

The San Diego Zoo's first vet was hired in 1929, thirteen years after the Zoo opened, and Dr. Schroeder, later the director, became clinical veterinarian in 1932. Today the Zoo has one of the largest veterinary staffs of any zoo in the world. There are two vets at the Wild Animal Park, and three vets, two pathologists, and a full research department at the Zoo.

The Zoo's animal health facilities are the most comprehensive of any in the zoo world. A new two-story hospital, the Jennings Center for Zoological Medicine, constructed at a cost of $1.2 million garnered from bequests, corporate and individual contributions, and local and national grants (named for its principal benefactor, Joseph B. Jennings), opened in 1978. The facilities include a treatment room, a pharmacy, a large X-ray room, an intensive-care room, an oxygen therapy unit, an isolation room with a separate ventilation system, a clinical pathology laboratory, a surgical prep room, a surgery room, and a recovery room with padded walls and floor designed to minimize injuries caused by the confusion of animals coming out of anesthesia. A second-floor observation area in the medical library permits visiting professionals and students to view surgical procedures.

The Zoo's first hospital, the Zoological Hospital and Biological Research Institute, built in 1926 at a cost of $50,000, was one of Dr. Wegeforth's great dreams. It housed a surgery room, a treatment room, and an X-ray room, and was exemplary in its day, but was finally inadequate to the needs of the growing Zoo. Today it houses the research department.

The veterinarians' jobs require tremendous dedication. The vets often have to work long days or go into the Zoo for emergencies during the middle of the night. Little is known about the medical care of exotic animals, and discovering effective ways of treating them is at once difficult and fascinating.

Since most animals in the Zoo are not handleable, a veterinarian usually has to sedate a sick animal or put it in a "squeeze cage" with walls or bars that contract to restrain it. All the drugs that are so valuable for treating humans and domestic animals are also used for treating exotics, but less is known of their effects on wild species. We don't know the proper dosages for unusual animals, and the wrong drug can produce a fatal reaction. A vet who's medicating or anesthetizing an exotic is often performing a medical first, and can only make educated guesses about dosage, based on the records of successful treatments of related animals.

It is the vets' responsibility to devise diets that will keep the animals in good health. In developing a diet for a particular species, they consider its food preferences in the wild, the known nutritional requirements of related species, availability, perishability, and economy. If it's not possible to provide animals with the food they would eat in the wild, nutritionally adequate substitutes must be supplied. At the Zoo, anteaters and aardvarks, which eat ants or termites in nature, are fed a blended mixture of milk, meat, and vitamins, which they slurp up with their tongues.

Vast quantities of food are necessary to sustain the animals at the Zoo and Wild Animal Park. The total daily output of the Zoo's animal food commissary includes about 510 pounds of grains and seeds; 450 pounds of Pacific mackerel; 25 pounds of anchovies; 300 pounds of frozen processed meat meal; 2,000 mealworms; 325 crickets; 1½ pounds of earthworms; 1,500 pounds of pelletized foods; 1,000 pounds of baled Sudan and alfalfa hay; 85 pounds of frozen horsemeat; 15 pounds of beef leg bones; 20 dozen eggs; 150 pounds of carrots; four boxes of apples; six cases of lettuce; 29 pounds of onions; 2½ crates of oranges, and 30 mice. The daily food bill runs to about $825, or $300,000 a year. The daily output of the food warehouses at the Wild Animal Park includes two tons of alfalfa pellets; two tons of hay; 600 pounds of assorted grains and seeds; three cases of assorted fruits and vegetables, and 120 pounds of processed meat meal, at a cost of about $700 a day.

The diets of many species are supplemented with plants that grow on the grounds of the Zoo and Park. The blossoms of the eucalyptus trees are fed to some of the Zoo's birds. The spathes, or flowered stocks, of palm are also fed to birds, while the fronds and fruit are fed to the elephants. Bamboos are food for the bongo, and the trunks and leaves of bananas are fed to the Galápagos tortoises, gorillas, and elephants. Acacia is used as browse for the okapis and giraffes and is cut up and fed to lemurs, apes, monkeys, and Galápagos tortoises. Hibiscus is fed to the wallabies, baboons, monkeys, and apes; eugenia to the monkeys, and cactus to the Galápagos tortoises. The leaves of the plant called giant bird of paradise are fed to the monkeys, while the trunks are fed to the elephants.

Some visitors have expressed horror at seeing fresh-killed baby rabbits, mice, or chicks fed to the snakes at the Zoo. Many zoos feed such animals out of sight of visitors, but I think that's wrong. Some animals—like people—live on other animals. A snake eats rodents, and if you want to show a snake in a zoo, you've got to supply it with rodents. Animals are fed live prey only when it's essential to maintain an animal. Some snakes, for example, will eat only live rodents, and generally they are fed out of sight of the public, because it necessitates too much explanation.

The postmortem examination performed whenever an animal dies at the Zoo or Wild Animal Park is primarily intended to determine the cause of death and aid in the development of preventive medical techniques. In addition, the information gathered during postmortems enables the vets to evaluate the effectiveness of their medical treatments and the adequacy of the animals' diets. Many zoos now share their veterinary data with one another. Data on animals' responses to anesthesia, diagnostic procedures, medical therapy, and surgery are accumulating at an unprecedented rate. But there are still many unknowns.

Many recent advances in zoological medicine involve the application of sophisticated medical techniques developed for humans to animals. Veterinary ophthalmology is one specialty that has been refined in the past decade. In 1976, a nine-month-old cheetah and an eight-year-old Siberian tiger at the Zoo, both suffering from cataracts in both eyes, underwent surgery, which was performed by Dr. Kirk Gelatt, a veterinary ophthalmologist at the University of Minnesota College of Veterinary Medicine in St. Paul.

184

Oral and dental health is important to the overall health of animals, since it is essential to their ability to assimilate their carefully planned diets. Dr. David A. Fagan, a dentist, is employed by the Zoo as a consultant-clinician, applying the latest achievements in the field of human dentistry to veterinary medicine. With a grant from the Zoological Society and working in cooperation with Dr. Phil Robinson, director of veterinary services, Dr. Fagan has developed a comprehensive mobile veterinary dental care unit that eliminates dependence on a stationary operating site. Early in 1977, it was determined that the intermittent sinus problems that had for years plagued Bob, the Zoo's male Bornean orangutan, were caused by an abscessed molar, and he underwent successful dental surgery. The same year, the Zoo's rare female maned wolf underwent surgery for severe gum disease; the pygmy chimp Linda, mother of seven of the twenty-two pygmy chimps in captivity, was treated for a broken front tooth, and a female north Chinese leopard with a severely destructive form of periodontal disease underwent root canal therapy and surgery.

The efforts of the veterinarians at the Zoo and Wild Animal Park are complemented by the work of the research staff. The Zoo's research director is Dr. Kurt Benirschke, a medical doctor who teaches at the University of California at San Diego Medical School. His field is genetics, and he's done some very notable research during his tenure.

A new bird-sexing technique developed by the Zoo's

research department is one recent advancement. In many bird species, there is no sexual dimorphism—males and females look alike—but of course, if two males or two females are paired, they won't breed. While sex could be determined by measuring hormone levels of the blood, many species of birds can't withstand the stress of having blood samples taken. To deal with these problems, the research department's endocrinology laboratory developed a technique for determining the sex of birds by measuring the levels of male and female sex hormones—testosterone and estrogen—in their fecal material. One fact learned as a consequence was both important and slightly embarrassing. For years, the Zoo had had no success in breeding kiwis. Indeed, the new sexing technique revealed that both of the Zoo's kiwis were males. Since then, two females have been obtained, though so far breeding has still not occurred.

The research department has also learned to determine if animals such as antelope are of the same subspecies through chromosome analysis of small blood samples. One species of antelope may include six subspecies, and as a result of this research, the Zoo can maintain pure strains by keeping those animals that are most alike together for reproduction.

After a year on the horse ranch, Jane and I moved to a house in Lemon Grove that had yard space for my dogs and corral space for my horses, and we lived together for two more years. Because Jane was a vet, we spent six months looking after one very special house guest, a cuddly-looking baby koala covered with silvery gray fur.

Koalas, often called "koala bears," are not really bears at all, though that's what seventeenth-century explorers of their native Australia believed them to be. And it's easy to understand why, for though they're only about two feet long, they have a bearlike form, are covered with woolly fur, and have the beadlike eyes and large dark nose of a child's teddy bear. But they are marsupials—mammals that bear their young in pouches, like kangaroos and wallabies.

Koalas are almost completely arboreal—they have clawed toes well divided for grasping, and live in the tops of eucalyptus trees. Their sole diet consists of leaves from these trees, and they drink little water; "koala" is Aborigine for "no drink." Young koalas, barely three-quarters of an inch long at birth, nurse for about six months in the marsupial pouch, and then ride on their mothers' backs until they are about a year old.

Koalas were once abundant throughout eastern Australia, but as a consequence of excessive hunting, they are now rare except in certain coastal regions of Queensland and today they are rigidly protected by law. Australia has always been highly selective in regard to export of any native wildlife, and a total ban on the export of koalas was enacted in the 1960's.

The San Diego Zoo is perhaps more closely identified with koalas than with any other single animal species. The Zoo's first koala was obtained in 1925, and its koala colony, the only one outside of Australia, was established in 1959, when a male and two females, each with an infant in her pouch, were received. The colony prospered for almost a decade, but then reproduction halted. The Zoo's koalas continued to set records for longevity in captivity with each passing year, but no young were born after 1968. A possible explanation is that inbreeding among the original small group eventually caused reproduction to cease; the trio of adult animals might have been too small a genetic pool to assure the long-term existence of the colony. In view of Australia's ban on the export of koalas, the 1976 death of Teddy, the Zoo's last male, seemed to seal the doom of San Diego's koala colony.

Teddy had appeared in some of the Australian airline's "I hate Qantas" television commercials that had made koalas beloved by millions of Americans, and among the expressions of concern that followed his death was an offer from the airline to try to help replace him. After a meeting between Australian officials and K. C. Lint, by then the Zoo's curator emeritus, and Dr. Phil Robinson, the Zoo's chief veterinarian, the Australian government agreed to waive the export ban on a one-time-only basis and present six koalas to the Zoo as a Bicentennial gift to the American people.

The likelihood of successful reproduction in San Diego was a major criterion for the selection of the four fe-males—Audrey, Pepsi, Matilda, and Coke—and two males—Cough Drop and Waltzing—that were flown to the Zoo in July 1976. All were from Australia's Lone Pine Sanctuary, where Cough Drop was the second best sire in the colony. Arrangements were made for the delicate cargo to make the 8,000-mile journey in passenger com-partments, in two crates (three animals per crate), each occupying three economy class seats. Qantas flew them from Australia to San Francisco, where a domestic carrier picked them up for the trip to San Diego. There was great excitement at the Zoo when the long-awaited koalas ar-rived and joined the Zoo's two surviving females, and the excitement was compounded when it was learned that Audrey and Pepsi had arrived with babies in their pouches.

In honor of their arrival, the Zoo constructed a new

$110,000 koala enclosure featuring an elevated, shaded viewing platform and landscaped with grassy lawn under eucalyptus trees and other native Australian foliage. A male and a female were placed on display in the visitors' viewing area, while the other koalas were semi-isolated in the adjacent Koala House, in order to encourage reproduction. From the elevated walkway, visitors could peek into the house, which consisted of a series of connecting low-walled rooms that allowed a koala to be isolated if necessary or to roam at will through the entire 1,700-square-foot area. All the rooms were equipped with climbing trees.

But tragedy soon visited the koala colony. In November, Audrey died of a combination of intestinal inflammation and virus infection, but her baby, a male named Gum Drop, survived.

Because he needed round-the-clock attention, Jane brought Gum Drop home to raise. He looked just like an adult koala, but was small enough to hold in two hands; he weighed just a pound and a half. We had a little eucalyptus branch in the house for him, and Jane brought home various kinds of fresh eucalyptus for him every single day. For the three months he lived with us, the house always smelled like eucalyptus.

Having one of the only koalas in America in your home might seem like a nifty conversation piece, but we didn't really want anybody to know we had Gum Drop, because we didn't want anybody to try to steal him. We couldn't let anybody in the house to see him or play with him, anyway, for fear he might catch some kind of virus, so his presence made the house kind of off-limits for company. Koalas are nocturnal, and Gum Drop slept most of the day and was active in the late afternoon and evening.

He was really a very quiet animal, but he grew a bit more active as he got older, and sometimes he played with the dogs, sitting on the back of one, holding on to its fur and riding around.

Not long after Gum Drop went back to the Zoo, two domestic ferrets became frequent visitors to our house. A newcomer to San Diego had moved them with him from Colorado, but when he learned that the California Fish and Game Department prohibited their maintenance as pets, he donated them to the Zoo. It was often convenient for me to keep them at home so that when I needed animals to take to lectures, I'd have them handy. I had to obtain a permit for them from California Fish and Game, which doesn't want ferrets loose because if they proliferate they might destroy native birds and threaten the poultry industry. In order to qualify, I had to have the ferrets neutered.

Ferrets have long slinky bodies with short, squatty legs, like minks. One of mine was a dark brown-black with a characteristic black mask around the eyes, and the other was albino—a yellowish white, with pink eyes, nose, and claws. Members of the Mustelidae family, which includes minks, skunks, weasels, and ermines, ferrets have a scent gland and exude a very peculiar, musty odor. They're also extremely inquisitive.

One day when I came back from riding in the mountains, I found the doors of the house standing open and mops out by the back door. As I drove in the truck and trailer, Jane came running out, calling, "The ferret's gone!" She had turned both ferrets loose to play in the laundry room, and they had chewed through the hose carrying water to the washing machine and flooded the room. Then the brown one, Sylvester, had crawled up through the dryer vent leading outside the house and disappeared.

I felt terrible. I had to have a permit to keep the ferrets because they were not supposed to be running loose, and now Sylvester was running around somewhere—who knew where—in the neighborhood. He wouldn't hurt anything, but I was more worried that he might get hurt himself.

To make matters worse, I had promised to take the ferrets on "The Tonight Show" the following week. I started calling all over the Zoo, trying to find another ferret that I could take on the show. Through some strange coincidence, a ferret had just been donated, and I was told I could use it as soon as it passed the quarantine that every animal that enters the Zoo undergoes to insure that it's not carrying any disease. I couldn't believe how lucky I was.

A couple of days later, some kids who lived down the street were playing near our house, and they asked me if I was the lady who worked at the Zoo. When I said I was, they told me very proudly that they'd just donated an animal to the Zoo. "They said it was a ferret," they told me. "We found it in the front yard, playing with our cat." Sure enough, when I picked up the quarantined ferret, it was Sylvester. I'd doubted I'd ever see him again, and it had never occurred to me that anyone would turn such a tame animal in at the Zoo, but he's still with me, living in a big cage in my office, a perennial favorite at my lectures.

During the years I lived with Jane, I sometimes wondered whether I had made a mistake when I gave up my early ambition to be a veterinarian. I also gained an appreciation of the pressures of the job—the phone would ring during dinner or in the middle of the night, and Jane would be off to the Zoo to take care of an emergency.

On one occasion, she was called in because Sumithi, the elephant I had worked with in the Children's Zoo, had fallen into the moat surrounding the elephant enclosure and couldn't right herself. Jane had bales of hay piled in the moat to prop Sumithi up and finally used a rope and a forklift to get her back on her feet—zoo vets often need to think fast to deal with such unprecedented problems. Many times I envied Jane her experiences, but I also came to understand that it takes a very special person to make a good zoo vet.

17

Ambassador at Large

At the end of the summer of 1974, I left the Park and returned to full-time work in the PR department. Red had already returned to work as a keeper there, while Don McLennan stayed at the Park to run the elephant show. The schedule of my activities as goodwill ambassador steadily expanded to include hosting famous Zoo visitors and traveling to other zoos around the country.

When First Lady Betty Ford visited the Zoo in May 1975, I helped show her around. Before her visit, those of us who were going to be close to her had to provide our social security numbers and driver's license numbers for security clearance, and the morning of her visit we were given identifying buttons to wear. When I was with her, we were surrounded at all times by Secret Service men (every one of them so good-looking that I started to won-

194

der if it was a requirement for the job). When we got to the elephants, I took Mrs. Ford right into the enclosure. It's nice, in my job, to have animals that can be safely handled, so that when you want to bring special guests in, you have something that you can show them. Mrs. Ford was very gracious and friendly, and she really seemed to enjoy the elephants, but photographers kept pushing me out of the way to get at her, and my tendency in such a situation is to step back rather than fight. So I kept finding myself clear at the end of the line, with Mrs. Ford, whom I was supposed to be guiding, way up ahead, separated from me by twenty people.

There's always a tremendous amount of preparatory work involved when a major political figure visits the Zoo. When Emperor and Empress Hirohito of Japan visited later the same year, security was even more stringent. I believe there had been a threat on Hirohito's life not long before, and anyway, the emperor is generally less accessible than an American president. There were security people on the roofs, overhead in the Skyride buckets, and surrounding the entire area that Hirohito visited.

Two days before the emperor's visit, Carole Towne, then the Zoo's public relations director, issued a four-page memo to all the Zoo personnel involved. We were informed of the emperor's scheduled arrival time, but were cautioned not to publicize it to visitors or callers. Elaborate plans were spelled out for the closing off of certain Zoo roadways and parking areas, the issuance of security identification, the laying of a red carpet, and the presentation of Zoo dignitaries to the emperor. Twenty grounds people were requested to sweep the area the emperor would see early on the day of his visit. Provision was made for the establishment of a police command post in a warehouse, and a communications center for the Japanese was set up in the Zoo's board room. Some 250 reporters and photographers were expected, and instructions for accommodating them were also provided.

The emperor and his party—enough people for a fifteen-car motorcade—were to see the kiwis, the okapis, the koalas, and the hummingbirds, and the memo outlined plans for their visit to each enclosure in great detail, even down to suggesting that Red Thomas, who was to show a koala to the emperor, wear a bright shirt to lend color to his tan uniform, because the *San Diego Union* would be trying for a color photograph. Plans to present the emperor with the decorated egg of a Darwin's rhea—an ostrichlike bird native to South America—had not yet been approved. "In any case," the memo noted, "it will have to be checked by the Secret Service and then attended to by one employee until the time of presentation." With all this preparation, the emperor was scheduled to spend just forty minutes at the Zoo.

Jimmy Carter visited the Zoo in September 1976, at the height of his campaign for the presidency. We knew in advance that at least 200 press people would be accompanying him, which meant that it would be difficult to move him around, so we decided to put some animals in a carry-all and tell Carter about them in front of the press. The first thing Carter did was get up on the tailgate of the carry-all and give a speech, and when he was done, we showed him the animals. It was hard to see or hear, and the press people kept pushing, but despite the commotion and excitement, it never really struck me that I might be talking to the next president of the United States.

Entertainment personalities also get personal tours from the Zoo's PR department, provided they call in advance and someone is free to accommodate them. I've shown around Ed McMahon, John Denver, Joan Rivers, and David Brenner. Because these people are so often before the public, we want them to have a favorable impression of the Zoo and Park.

As part of my growing PR responsibilities, I began to do more traveling as the Zoo's representative, visiting other zoos throughout the country, speaking before their local zoological societies, and sometimes giving press interviews about what goes into a good zoo and how modern zoos cooperate with one another for the preservation of endangered animals. My travels acquainted me with the workings of a variety of large and small animal operations, and of course, there were always new and exciting wild creatures to see.

When I visited the Hattiesburg Kamper Park Zoo in Hattiesburg, Mississippi, just outside of Jackson, I saw an elephant that had been raised with a goat as a companion. The two had a tremendous friendship, but every time the goat walked away, even if it was only fifty feet, the elephant had a fit. She'd scream, throw things at the goat, and run back and forth in her pen until the goat came back. Sometimes she'd grab it with her trunk and pull it into the enclosure, then wrap her trunk around the goat and fondle it. If she wanted the goat in a particular part of the pen, she'd nudge it there with her foot. The goat was very accommodating, but the elephant was almost totally dependent on it.

One of my trips took me to Waco, Texas, to address the annual meeting of their zoological society. During my visit, I went to the McCracken Arabian Ranch, one of the largest and best-known Arabian ranches in the United

States. I went through the barns and saw the horses, and they brought their prize stallion out into their beautiful indoor ring so I could see him work. Then they offered to let me ride him. I remember thinking, "I don't know if I even want to get up on a half-million dollar horse. With my luck, he'll trip and break a leg." But I did ride him, and it was a thrill just to sit on such a magnificent animal.

Before I visited Bismarck, North Dakota, I spoke with the zoo director on the phone. "I'm really looking forward to seeing your zoo," I told him, and he said, "Honey, our zoo's under six feet of snow right now." Indeed, in Bismarck, the temperature was twenty degrees below zero and there was snow all over the ground, and the animals were all housed in barns and temporary pens. The people at the Bismarck Zoo gave me a snowmobile suit, and I wore it most of the time I was there.

Still, I had a great time. The director was a charming fellow, Mark Christianson, who is now retired. He took me out in a car to look for pronghorn antelope, which were in danger of starving because of the snow. The zoo people took food out to them, and if things got too bad, they intended to rescue them and bring them into the zoo. Despite the weather, the antelope were able to run, and they can run as fast as cheetahs, sixty to sixty-five miles an hour. It was incredible to watch them spring into the air and through the snow.

Wherever I've traveled, the local people have been generous and hospitable, but Art May, who owns a camera shop in Bismarck, did one of the nicest things anybody's ever done for me. He was teasing me about my pocket camera, but I assured him that it was fine for my purposes and that I didn't have the money for a more professional camera. And he handed me a complete 35-millimeter outfit.

That camera was a very special gift, for it has enabled me to record all the travels my job has afforded me since.

During the first day of my visit to Fort Wayne, Indiana, where I was to address the annual zoological society meeting, the director showed me around the zoo. As we walked through the education department, we happened on an aquarium filled with large tropical millipedes, which grow to a length of about twelve inches. I'd never seen such millipedes before; the San Diego Zoo doesn't do much with insects, spiders, or other arthropods. The millipedes were handleable, and I thought they made an outstanding display for the education department—a child would be fascinated by their movement, because they have many body segments, each with two pairs of legs. I'm always on the lookout for animals that are relatively small and easy to keep, but unusual and interesting. And despite my distaste for handling such creatures, I don't mind looking at them through glass. So I raved to the education director and zoo director about how wonderful the millipedes were.

A few nights later, I spoke at the Fort Wayne Zoological Society's annual formal dinner-dance. After my presentation, as a thank-you gift, I was presented with—of all things—a millipede. And the first thing they did was pull it out of its jar and hand it to me.

There must have been two or three hundred zoological society members sitting there, all very pleased to think that I was getting a millipede from the Fort Wayne Zoo. I didn't want to seem ungrateful, so I tried to show great appreciation, and I did touch the millipede, then put it back into the jar as quickly as possible and ended my lecture. Afterward, everybody wanted me to show it around. After all, I'd just talked about all the animals I'd handled, and here was this millipede I had said was really neat. As soon as I could, I ran it up to my room and locked the door, and every time someone asked, I apologized, "Oh, I'm sorry, but the millipede's upstairs."

After I got back to San Diego, I decided to take the millipede to "The Tonight Show." When I started preparing, I discovered that there was very little published information about millipedes, particularly about the type they'd given me. There was practically nothing in our library, so I went to San Diego's Natural History Museum, where there are drawers full of collected insect and arthropod specimens. The people there helped me establish the scientific name of the particular millipede I had so that I could pursue my research.

The man who was helping me mentioned that many people confuse millipedes with centipedes, since both have many legs and they look somewhat alike. They are related, but centipedes have one pair of legs on each body segment, are equipped with poison fangs, and eat insects, worms, and slugs. Some even capture toads, lizards, and snakes. "I happen to have a live centipede here," the man told me. "I'd be willing to let you take it to show the difference between the two."

I took the centipede home that night. I already had the millipede there, because I was practicing handling it, just as I had the tarantula. Because the centipede was poisonous, I wasn't going to handle it; I would just show it in its glass jar.

When a friend came to visit that night, I told him to look at the centipede. He stood shaking the jar, saying he didn't see anything. "You can't miss it—it's a big centipede," I assured him. "It's under the shavings. Just keep shaking the jar." But he said, "No, it's not there." I took the jar from him and started turning it around, and I couldn't find it either. Finally, we took the lid off and took some of the shavings out, but the centipede was nowhere to be found.

Suddenly I felt very threatened—somewhere loose in my house was an eight-inch centipede. I had to get up early the next morning and drive up to Los Angeles for the taping, and it was getting late, but I wasn't about to go to bed with a centipede loose in my house. We searched for about half an hour before I spotted two feelers and a head sticking up out of the garbage disposal. The centipede was lurking down under the lip. I got a pair of forceps and let my friend use them to grab hold of the centipede and put it back in the jar. We put a new cover over the top, and I left it out on the back step till it was time to leave the next morning.

One of the trips my job has enabled me to take really amounted to a kind of working vacation. In the fall of 1975, the Royal Viking Line, which is based in San Francisco, invited me to be guest lecturer on either their trans-Panama Canal cruise or their Alaskan cruise. Every ship in the line has a very beautiful, fully-equipped theater, and each morning they're at sea, a lecturer makes a presentation. Since I'd been busy all summer doing elephant shows, I thought it would be fun to go someplace where I could have summer weather, so I chose the Canal cruise.

The cruise, which lasted nearly four weeks, went from New York to Fort Lauderdale, through the Caribbean and the Canal, up to Acapulco and on to Long Beach. I was allowed to bring one person along, and I decided to take my mother, because I knew she'd get a big kick out of it.

On various days, I talked about African animals, zoo babies, elephant training, my television experiences, the

Zoo, and the Wild Animal Park. I'd give a lecture in the morning and work that night on the next day's lecture.

I especially enjoyed the week in the Caribbean, and I learned a lot going through the Panama Canal. In Mexico I went water-skiing in Acapulco and skin-diving in Puerto Vallarta.

Of course, between all my trips, personal appearances in and around San Diego continued to be a major part of my job. One of the lectures I gave in early 1976 was at a luncheon of the Exchange Club, a service organization to which my father belongs. As usual, I was asked to bring along an animal, so I decided to take a Jackson's chameleon. It comes from Africa, and it's an astonishing, almost prehistoric-looking animal. About nine inches long, it's a brilliant green color and has three horns protruding from the end of its nose. Because it's a tree dweller, its toes are separated for grasping, and it has a long prehensile or grasping tail, by which it can hang. The chameleon's eyes rotate independently, so that one can look forward while the other looks backward.

One of the most fascinating things about the chameleon is the way it eats. Though it moves very slowly, it catches insects with its tongue, which is almost as long as its body and has a sticky pad at the end. The chameleon's eyes rotate until it spots an insect and then, in an instant, its tongue darts out and catches it.

I wanted to show the Exchange Club how a chameleon eats, so just before going to the hotel where the luncheon was to be held, I stopped at the reptile house and asked them to put a couple of crickets in a little paper box.

After lunch, I displayed the chameleon, and then tried, while still holding it, to open the box and grab a cricket. I feel the same way about crickets as I do about all other insects—squeamish—and somehow I dropped the box. And instead of two crickets, the box was packed with maybe two *hundred* crickets, which were now jumping all over the room, on the table, in the lunches, and on the wall. Instead of hearing a lecture on the Zoo, my well-dressed hosts spent the rest of the hour on their hands and knees, capturing crickets with their water glasses.

When I make appearances as the Zoo's goodwill ambassador, I like to think I do something of value, making people aware of the pressures on wildlife today and of the importance of supporting good zoos. But the other side of the story is how good the job has been to me, enabling me to travel and meet a number of famous and fascinating people. A decade in this job has given me more memorable experiences than I could have hoped for in a lifetime of work.

18

Show Biz

Just as I use entertainment to communicate with people via television, animal shows at the Zoo are designed to attract people through entertainment. People begin to appreciate animals more quickly when they see an animal with tremendous personality, like Carol, perform, and it would take long study of elephants in the wild or at the Zoo and Park to see all the behaviors that Carol is trained to perform on command. Once people have been attracted by the entertaining aspect of the Zoo's animal shows, they can be educated about the Zoo's more serious goal of protecting endangered species.

At the beginning of the summer of 1976, I was asked at the last minute to put together a new show for Wegeforth Bowl. I had a very short time to create the whole thing, and there was lots of pressure, because the Zoo started advertising the show heavily through TV and radio commercials, big newspaper display ads, and even billboards on the freeways—"See Joan Embery live at the San Diego Zoo!"

Carol was shipped down from the Wild Animal Park, but another elephant had recently knocked her around, bruising her hips so badly that she couldn't even walk, so I couldn't work her. I would have liked to teach her some new behaviors and let her get used to working in Wegeforth again, but I couldn't put her onstage until two days before the show opened, anyway, because there was construction to be done. Carol had grown so much since her last appearances in Wegeforth Bowl that we had to have a wall torn out and a much larger door to the stage built for her.

Because I was developing the show on my own, I needed to hire another person to work as my backup, taking animals on and off the stage and helping to feed and care for them. My goal was to train my assistant to be self-sufficient, so that he or she could take over if I had to be away. I went through a lot of job applications on file at the Zoo, interviewed about ten people, and finally picked Kathy Marmack, an attractive girl about three years younger than I. Kathy was lively and outgoing and seemed like she'd get along well with other people, and she had some experience working with domestic animals. I didn't expect to find anyone who was familiar with elephants and cougars and wolves—Cody and Rufus would also be in the show—but I did want someone who had some background with animals, and when I interviewed her, Kathy was working for a veterinarian.

I worried a bit when she started working with me, because I'd never felt so directly responsible for another person's safety before. I had three weeks to teach Kathy about handling and training animals and to get her accustomed to handling a full-grown wolf, a full-grown cougar, and a sizable elephant. Cody weighed about 125 pounds by then, and Carol, who was nine years old, was seven feet tall and weighed 4,500 pounds, though she was not full grown. At maturity she'd be eight to ten feet tall and weigh between eight and ten thousand pounds.

I kept telling Kathy to discipline this enormous animal, not to let her get away with things. When it comes to training, beginners—especially if they're animal lovers—tend to start out saying things like, "Carol, would you please pick up your foot?" instead of saying, "Pick up your foot!" in a demanding way. When Kathy did that, Carol would look at her as if to say, "What are you going to do about it if I don't?"

Kathy's moment of truth came the first week on the job. I had told her again and again that she must never let herself get caught between Carol and a wall and that she mustn't go around Carol without a bull hook, especially because she was just starting out. She might be able to do that after a few months, when Carol had gotten to know her and had learned a little respect for her, but in the beginning, if Kathy said "Move over!" and Carol didn't want to cooperate, she might not be able to control her without the bull hook. Even a well-trained elephant may stand up to a new handler, and it's up to the handler to establish position and dominance for himself.

While Kathy was raking and picking up Carol's manure, she leaned her bull hook against the wall for a moment, and immediately Carol, who was chained nearby, reached over and grabbed Kathy's rake with her trunk. Before Kathy had even reacted, Carol grabbed her and tried to push her against the wall. I had already told Kathy many times that she should always be firm with Carol, and she remembered. "Trunk down!" she commanded. And Carol put her trunk down. "Back up!" Kathy ordered. And Carol backed up. That really got the point across. And it was a long time before Kathy went walking around again without her bull hook.

That same week, I had to give a lecture, so I left Kathy for the morning to feed and take care of the animals alone. "Now, are you sure you can handle this?" I asked her before I left, and Kathy said, "Yeah, I'll be really careful, I promise." But when I got back to the Zoo at midday, the people in the office greeted me with the news that Kathy had been taken to the hospital. I'm sure I turned white. "What was it, the elephant?" I asked. "Oh my God—the elephant? The cat? The wolf?" I didn't give anybody time to tell me that after she'd finished feeding the animals, Kathy had gone into my office to look for something and cracked her head on a drawer of the file cabinet.

I had two new animals for the show, a guanaco and a red-tailed hawk. The guanaco, Frisky, came from the Children's Zoo. Guanacos belong to the Cameloid family, which also includes llamas, alpacas, vicuñas, and dromedary and Bactrian camels. Frisky looked very much like a llama. She had the same long, fragile-looking neck, large limpid eyes, long ears, and pert expression. Both llamas and guanacos have a split lip, and while the senior girls in the Children's Zoo used to tease the beginners by telling them that the cameloids had had their teeth knocked out, the truth is that they don't have any upper teeth. Llamas come in all colors, while guanacos come in one basic color pattern, an apricot-colored coat with a black or dark gray muzzle. They are close in size, but llamas, about three-and-a-half feet high at the shoulder, are a little bigger than guanacos, and a guanaco's head is smaller and more pointed at the nose, more chiseled looking, than a llama's.

Guanacos are semidomesticated in South America, where they're maintained as beasts of burden. If handled from infancy, a guanaco can easily be trained to a halter, almost like a pony, so Frisky was a good animal for the kind of public appearances I make, as well as for the show.

There was one big drawback, however. Cameloids spit. If people tease them or irritate them, they spit in their faces. Cameloids are ruminants, which means they have four-chambered stomachs, and like cows, they eat, then regurgitate their food, chew it, and swallow it again. Nothing smells worse than guanaco or llama spit—it's regurgitated food—and their aim is deadly accurate. We had to groom Frisky every morning for the show, but she hated to be brushed, and every morning she kicked and spat.

Guanacos are not particularly smart, and they're stubborn, but it's fairly easy to train them with food rewards. I taught Frisky to "cush," or lie down, by tapping the front of her legs and pulling down on her halter until she kneeled. Guanacos are very good jumpers, and I taught her to take fences, too. It was just a matter of running with her up to the jump and letting her go over.

We got our red-tailed hawk, Anastasia, from Dick Todd, a San Diego man who rehabilitates a lot of local animals and turns them loose. She was what falconers call an eyas—a young bird—and was found in a nest when it was taken down off a power pole by San Diego Gas and Electric. Dick raised her by hand.

Anastasia was brown, with an orange-red tail. When full grown, she was about eighteen inches long and had a four-foot wingspan. She had big dark eyes, long talons, and a long beak. Most people think the beak is dangerous, but hawks hunt and defend themselves with their talons. The talons have a locking mechanism that goes into action when the hawk picks up prey, and when Anastasia got upset, she would clamp down and lock her feet into my arm. I usually wore a big leather glove when I handled her, and sometimes when I forgot it, her talons actually pierced my skin.

Dick Todd taught me how to handle Anastasia. When I got her, she was trained to sit on a perch, and eventually she learned to sit quietly on my hand while I talked about her, in itself considerable training for a hawk. A hawk is handled by "jesses," leather leg straps attached to a swivel that has a three-foot leash running through the other end. The bird can hop up and down, but if it tries to fly, the leash keeps it from getting away. Usually. Twice when I was showing Anastasia outside the Zoo, the leash somehow came loose. The first time, I was speaking before one of the service clubs in Imperial Beach, a San Diego suburb, and Anastasia flew up to the top of the chandelier, where she sat for a good part of the luncheon. When she finally flew down to the piano, I captured her. She got away again at a Sears parking lot sale and landed high in a big tree in the middle of the parking lot. As usual at those sales, the lot was jammed with people, so a large audience watched me climb the tree to reach her leash and pull her back down.

As the summer progressed, Anastasia learned to fly from Kathy to me. Kathy would hold her and I'd toss a piece of food up, and she'd fly to get it. Hawks have telescopic vision and can see a tiny piece of food in the hand of a person 500 feet away. People often shoot birds like Anastasia to get a closer look at them, but in our shows, the audience had a chance to see Anastasia and appreciate her magnificent hunting ability without causing her any harm.

As always, Carol was the star of the show. When I talked about the difference between Asian and African elephants—the Asians' smaller ears are the most immediately recognizable difference—she would wiggle her ears. Then she would raise her trunk and "trumpet" or "talk." Standing on an eight-inch beam, she would balance, pick up her feet, change feet, and turn all the way around. Then she'd pick up a log and float it in the seal pool surrounding the stage, just as Asian work elephants drop logs in a river to float them to a mill. Sometimes she would do her still-popular painting routine or give a concert on, successively, harmonica, tambourine, and drums. After taking a bow, she'd skip to "The Baby Elephant Walk," then lift Kathy or me in her trunk, and finally stand on her hind legs and wave good-bye to the audience with her trunk.

The very first performance we gave was a special night preview of the summer show at a barbecue to which all the people with Zoo memberships were invited. We'd been scrambling to get the show ready as it was, and the Zoo gave us only short notice of the special performance. It was frightening for Kathy, who was not only just learning to work the animals, but who had never done any public speaking, to make her debut in front of an audience of Zoo members. We knocked ourselves out trying to get ready, and by the time the barbecue rolled around, we were keyed up and nervous. Few people have seen me when I couldn't eat, but I couldn't, and neither could Kathy.

When the show began, I introduced myself and launched into the narrative I'd prepared while Kathy went to get Cody, who was kept in a small room backstage. But somehow he had slipped into the adjacent room, where Kathy and I kept our things, and had gotten hold of all my clothes and ripped and chewed them to shreds. When Kathy opened the door, he flew at her, and she slammed the door in his face. When she reappeared without Cody, looking stunned, I knew that something was wrong, so I abandoned the audience and ran back to the room. There was Cody, crouched over my clothes, growling. I grabbed hold of a stick and swatted it at him, and he turned around and ran into the corner and sat there sulking. Then I grabbed my clothes and threw them out of the room, and Cody just sat and purred as though everything were fine. Poor Kathy had been terrified, but I knew Cody well, and I was more irritated than frightened. I grabbed his leash and took him onstage, and the show went on.

Things went smoothly while I showed Cody, Rufus, Frisky, and Anastasia, and when I was through talking about the hawk, I put her on her perch, tied her leash to it, and left it onstage, so people could look at her. We brought Carol out, and just as she began her routine on the balance beam, the hawk flew off her perch, knocking it over and spooking Carol. She got so flustered that she started trumpeting and flapping her ears in and out and almost bounced off the beam. Kathy ran over and put Anastasia back on her perch, but she jumped right off again. Carol's eyes were bulging out and her trunk was up and she was snorting, and every time the hawk got near her, Carol would swat at her.

That show seemed to go on forever. Kathy couldn't re-member her lines, but we didn't know what was going to happen next anyway, so we just had to ad-lib everything. The members who had seen some kind of special show year after year had come to expect perfection, but that night they got a real comedy of errors.

The new show gave Carol a regular audience again, and she loved it. She'd do anything to get a laugh out of people. One day when she was painting, she threw her brush accidentally—it flew out of her trunk and into the seal pool—and everybody laughed. For the next week, she threw her brush in the pool during every show. After I disciplined her for it, she'd wait till I wasn't looking, and then throw it in the pool.

During the finale of another performance, when Carol was lifting me, I lost my balance and she lost her grip and I fell to the ground. The audience was shocked—it was nearly a ten-foot fall—but Carol was even more dis-tressed. She started shrieking, wrapping her trunk around me and touching me to make sure I was okay.

I trained Carol to pick up a bucket of apples at the end of the show and carry them back to her bull pen. One day, Cody started giving us trouble at the end of the show, and while Kathy and I were busy with him, Carol picked up her bucket and left. She carried it back to her bull pen, and ordinarily she would have walked right in, but on this particular afternoon, she caught sight of some brand new banana trees, the pride and joy of the Zoo horticulturist. When we caught up with her, she was de-molishing the banana grove, having a ball screaming and pulling the shallowly rooted trees up and throwing them in the air. She must have destroyed thirty of them. I swear she had a big smirk on her face when I dragged her back to her bull pen. Kathy and I kind of propped some of the trees up, trying to reduce the obvious damage, but it was a pretty hopeless task.

After the last show each day, Kathy and I would take Carol to the Baskin-Robbins booth near Wegeforth Bowl. She'd put her trunk through the window and they'd hand her an ice cream cone, and she'd eat it whole. That was her favorite treat.

When the show closed at the end of the summer, the stagehand and I decided to give Kathy a dunking during the last performance, as a joke. Carol was going to pick Kathy up that day, and we positioned the tub Carol sat on so that when she tried to set Kathy back down onstage, she'd drop her into the seal pool instead. When Kathy hit the water, poor Carol thought she'd done something wrong, and she got scared and started barking. Everybody in the audience was laughing and screaming and yelling, and Carol just stood there and didn't know what to do.

Right after the show closed, I was asked to take Carol to perform during the half-time show of the St. Louis Cardinals–San Diego Chargers football game, the biggest Chargers game of the year. Carol was to do her entire routine, just as she did it at the Zoo, with a marching band behind her playing "The Baby Elephant Walk" and "Talk to the Animals." As usual when such a request is made, I was asked, "Can you do this?" It's often a hard decision, and in this case, I could end up with 48,000 people sitting there waiting to see an elephant that, if she got excited before the games, might not show. I couldn't predict just what Carol would do, because I'd never taken her to a football game before.

But I said yes, and then got busy ensuring that Carol

would in fact perform. I knew that if she was going to work during the football halftime, she was going to have to get used to the presence of a marching band. I found out that the Optimist Youth Band, made up of students from various San Diego high schools, practiced in the parking lot of the Zoo, so I telephoned all over town to find out when they practiced, and the next time they met, Kathy and I took Carol to rehearsal.

As we were walking her there, she was just fine, but the instant she caught sight of the band, her ears went straight out to the side and she did a 180-degree turn and tore across the parking lot, almost running over a brand-new Mercedes before we caught her. Clearly, she wasn't going to get anywhere near the band. All she wanted to do was run away, so we put hobbles on her front legs—kind of tied them together—so she couldn't run very far.

We needed to show Carol somehow that the band wasn't going to hurt her, so we chained her to a great big eucalyptus tree in the middle of the parking lot, started the band at the end of the lot, and marched them around her at a distance of about 500 feet. When that ceased to bother her, the band came within 400 feet, then 300, then 200—until at last they were marching around the tree in tight circles. It was a funny sight—this huge band going around and around an elephant chained to a tree—and it must have been astonishing to the musicians who thought they were going to be practicing for a football game to suddenly find themselves in a training session for an elephant. When Carol realized that the band was not going to hurt her, and began to accept the noise—for they were really very loud—we took the chains off and marched her around behind the band.

The day of the game, we took Carol to the stadium

ahead of time to practice with the band she'd actually be performing with. She was still a little nervous, because the music echoed so in the empty stadium. But when half-time came, the show went off without a hitch. Carol's performance was a big success, and our hosts were so pleased that they invited us back the following year.

With the Wegeforth show closed, I decided to give Anastasia her freedom. She had been fed a homogenized bird-of-prey diet at the Zoo, but I began teaching her to catch live prey by putting birds and rodents in her pen, which was about forty feet around, so she could fly and swoop down to catch them.

One of the Park employees with whom I worked, Justin, had an aunt who owned a big ranch in the San Pasqual Valley a couple of miles from the Park, and one beautiful fall day, he took Anastasia out there and turned her loose. She stayed around for a minute, and then took off, but for a long time after that, Justin would tell me that he'd seen her circling over the ranch.

I didn't have any regrets about losing her. Though zoos are necessary for the survival of many species, nothing compares to a wild and free existence. Anastasia had served the Zoo's educational purposes well through her role in our shows, and I was glad to see her free again.

19

My African Safaris

For many years, Keith Tucker, a local travel agent, had run African tours in cooperation with the Zoo. The Zoo advertised the tours to its members in order to provide them with a special activity, and in exchange the Zoo got to send an employee to Africa. I dreamed of going to Africa, but the chances of my going on one of the Zoo tours were slim, because top management people were always picked to go. Then in 1976, Keith Tucker asked me if I would like to put together a "Safari with Joan Embery." If enough people signed up, I'd go as tour leader. When the safari sold out, I was ecstatic.

The safari was to take us ·to Kenya and Tanzania, through a number of the game parks maintained by the national governments. There are wild animal parks all over the world, but most of the biggest and best-known are in Africa. The largest of the African parks, the Etosha Pan Nature Conservation Area in South-West Africa, covers 26,000 square miles. The Wild Animal Park in San Diego is 1,800 acres, or about 3 square miles, so even the smallest African park, at 20 square miles, is more than six times as big, and most are 100 square miles and up. While our Wild Animal Park was created out of southern California farmland, the African parks are existing natural areas. Occasionally, if there are few animals of a species in a certain area, animals are moved in from elsewhere as part of rehabilitation programs, but for the most part, the African parks are intended to preserve existing animal populations.

Naturally, this was to be a camera safari; there is no better souvenir to bring home from a trip to East Africa than a photograph of a beautiful wild animal living free. Our plans were to travel through the game parks from one lodge to another, making a morning game run, an afternoon game run, and occasionally a night game run in Jeeps or Land-Rovers, looking for animals with the help of a guide. Our lodgings would vary from hotels to huts to tents in camps.

My responsibilities were minimal—I had to check people in and out, keep track of luggage, and make contacts through the proper tour companies along the way. No one from the travel agency was accompanying us, and I was given ten pages of instructions on what to do if someone lost his passport, was injured, or became ill.

Twenty-two of us left San Diego on October 12 for the three-week trip. We flew to Africa via Frankfurt, Germany, where the curator of the beautiful Frankfurt Zoo gave us a personal tour. There I saw two animal species I'd never seen before—geranuks and giant forest hogs. Geranuks are antelope with extremely long necks, fine legs, and small heads. They're very delicate and have a giraffelike appearance, and unlike other antelope, which browse on the ground, they stand on their hind legs and browse from the tops of trees. Since my trip, we've acquired geranuks at the Wild Animal Park, and it's really something to see them balancing on their hind legs and eating from the acacias. The giant forest pigs were huge, almost gruesome-looking animals with hair all over their bodies. They weighed about 500 pounds each. There are none in zoos in this country, because it's illegal to import swine.

We flew from Frankfurt to Nairobi, and our safari began on October 17, with a drive into the foothills of Mt. Kenya. In four minibuses equipped with open photo hatches above the middle and backseats, we traveled through lush green countryside, past sisal and coffee plantations, tea gardens, and other agricultural land.

Our first stop was Wilderness Trails, a tented camp on a huge cattle ranch owned by Delia and David Craig. (During drought years that made farming difficult, the Craigs had established Wilderness Trails as a second source of income.) We camped there for two nights, within sight of Mt. Kenya, which is, at 17,040 feet, the highest mountain in Kenya and the second highest in Africa after Kilimanjaro. Fifteen glaciers surround its peak.

Tent camps were our most primitive accommodations during our safari, but in Africa, they really know how to travel "primitive." In the camps, servants did our laundry, awakened us every morning with tea, kept us supplied with fresh water, cleaned our tents, made our beds, and came regularly to spray for insects.

Wilderness Trails was especially luxurious. The tents, each of which held one or two cots, had thatched mats for floors. Each night, attendants brought us hot water bottles and little Thermoses of water with which we could brush our teeth. There was a bar in the big dinner tent, and the home-cooked food was outstanding.

Outside the back of each tent was a shower—a three-sided shelter with its open side facing and close to the tent. On the ground were boards over holes for the water to run into, and across the top was a branch holding a bucket with a shower head on it. When one of us was ready to shower, an African attendant heated water for the bucket over a fire.

There were no telephones at the ranch, just a short-wave radio for communication. When supplies were needed, the Craigs flew to Nairobi in their own plane.

The Craigs are committed to the preservation of wildlife and live in peaceful coexistence with the animals around them. Their cattle aren't fenced; they're herded by African workers.

The Craigs had once owned two ranches, but the Kenyan government had forced them to sell the other so that it could be divided into ten-acre small holdings and turned over to Kenyan families to be farmed. (The Craigs live with the constant threat that their second ranch may be taken over, too.) Unfortunately, when the first ranch was subdivided and cultivated, the wild animals were driven off. Whatever one's view of the political situation in Kenya, it is sadly inevitable that as Africans begin to farm more, they will destroy more areas where wildlife once thrived.

Except in a few remote areas of Africa where we traveled in four-wheel-drive vehicles, our minibuses took us out for two and sometimes three daily game runs. We rode through the parks accompanied by a professional guide

conversant with the animals, plants, history, and people of
the area. He and our drivers were well trained in sighting
and identifying wildlife.

There's an immeasurable difference between seeing a
leopard in a cage and being in the wild, not even knowing if there's a leopard in the forest, and suddenly seeing
one emerge from the brush. I loved never knowing what
we were going to see or how we were going to see it. I
loved knowing the animals hadn't been interfered with.
We at zoos can try all we want to duplicate nature, but
with our best efforts we can't even come close to matching
the natural habitat that is Africa.

Each game run lasted from an hour and a half to as
long as six hours. We covered rough ground, and it was
hot, but I went on just about every game run, because I
didn't want to miss a thing. Naturally, the biggest thrill
for me was seeing elephants. We saw them in groups
ranging anywhere from five to thirty animals—it was my
first chance to see baby elephants in their family groups—
and occasionally we saw lone bulls. We also saw how destructive elephants can be; they had completely stripped
some areas of trees.

Walking safaris were a special feature of Wilderness
Trails. Moving slowly and quietly, we had a close view
of birds and animals gathered at water holes and saw
things we couldn't see when we traveled in the minibuses—plants, insects, snakes, and the physical details of
the land. One afternoon, we were able to get amazingly
close to a big herd of elephants because we were down-
wind of them.

After leaving the Craigs' ranch, we drove south and
entered Mt. Kenya National Park, where we spent a night

in the forest of the Abedare Mountains at the Ark, a tree-house-type lodge situated over water holes where animals come throughout the night to drink. To enter, we climbed a long wooden staircase that was pulled up behind us. We stayed up for hours watching the animals, which couldn't see us since we were above them. If we got tired, we could go to our rooms to sleep, leaving word about the type of animals we particularly wanted to see, and if that species came in, the staff would ring an individual alarm to wake us. In the middle of the night, I was awakened, as I had requested, when a herd of elephants came in.

The next leg of our trip took us back toward Nairobi, down the escarpment of the Great Rift Valley, the world's largest valley, five thousand miles long. At the bottom, we spent an entire day at Mayer's Ranch, visiting a Masai "manyatta," or village. The Masai, very tall, slender, black people with elegant features, retain many ancient tribal customs. We saw their huts made of cow dung, and we watched their traditional dances and their sports, which originated as training for war—historically, the Masai were the greatest warriors in East Africa. The Masai shave their heads and put corks in holes in their ear lobes to stretch them and form big loops in which they wear bright bead earrings. When they're not wearing earrings, they fold their ear lobes up over the tops of their ears. I bought a lot of their beautiful beads.

From the Masai village we continued west to the Masai Mara Game Reserve, a northern extension of Tanzania's famed Serengeti National Park. There we spent three nights at Governor's Camp, a private tented camp, and did the most exciting game viewing of our whole tour. The Mara has one of the densest wildlife populations in

East Africa, and on our game runs it was easy to spot incredible numbers of animals.

Most of the kills I saw were in the Mara. Usually we spotted animals on the run, but we could sit and watch cats on a kill. If we saw another vehicle stopped, we'd often go see what its occupants were looking at, and it was usually a kill. Other times we were led to a kill by the sight of vultures circling overhead.

I'd read about kills and certainly I knew that predators kill other animals. Still, it was awesome to see a wild cat devouring its prey. The only times I'd ever seen animals dead at the Zoo, it was sad, but a kill inspired more complex feelings. The struggle for life—the struggle to find food, avoid predators, and survive droughts, floods, and fires—is a fact of daily existence for animals in the wild. Through reading, I had long been aware that nature has an almost cruel side. Some of the tour members were upset by the sight of a lion devouring a water buffalo, but I just didn't think of it as gory; it seemed natural in those surroundings.

We rarely saw an actual chase, but one day we were able to watch a cheetah hunting. We were out on a game run in a four-wheel-drive Land-Rover when we came across the cheetah and her two cubs, which, judging by their size, were two or three months old. She left them sitting in the open plains—there was little cover anywhere—and began stalking a group of between five and ten Thomson's gazelles, dainty antelope that have diagonal black stripes on their flanks and stand only about two feet tall. The cheetah had characteristic long legs, a long tail, and a small head, and crouching close to the ground, she made an impressive hunter. Within a few moments she started running toward a gazelle that had wandered away from the group. Usually, cheetahs rush their prey from a considerable distance and outrun them. But the gazelle eluded her. Cheetahs are the fastest of all four-legged creatures—they have been clocked at sixty-five miles an hour—but only over very short distances.

Then the cheetah rushed a second gazelle. The chase was so fast that even with four-wheel drive we couldn't keep up, so we didn't actually see her pull the gazelle down. When we caught up, she was dragging it back to her cubs. Then we saw a spotted hyena approach.

There was no fight. The cheetah became immediately submissive and just gave the gazelle to the hyena. Hyenas outweigh cheetahs, are extremely strong, with powerful jaws and teeth capable of splintering the heaviest bones, and are notorious for fighting for food. Cheetahs rely almost entirely on their feet when hunting—they beat their prey down with their forefeet before biting them through the neck—and their jaws are very weak. At that point, the cheetah was especially vulnerable because she was so tired. She went on back to her kittens, while the hyena devoured her hard-won prey.

At Governor's Camp, we were not supposed to go back and forth among the tents after dark without an armed guard, because the camp was in the middle of a section where cape buffalo grazed, and in the evening they came very close to the tents. Cape buffalo are ferocious looking—they have horns that wrap over the front of their heads—and indeed they are among the most aggressive and bad-tempered of animals. Though the buffalo around Governor's Camp were familiar with the activity in the camp, if one was startled, it might be provoked to charge.

222

One night when I was in the dinner tent, one of the people in my group asked me for a flashlight, and I ran back to my tent to get mine, forgetting all about the armed guard. I was on my way back to the dinner tent when I saw something move. I froze. Then I saw a huge figure and horns, and I realized I was standing no more than five feet from a cape buffalo the size of a huge bull. They're black, so they're almost invisible at night. He just looked at me as, very slowly, I backstepped all the way to my tent. I waited there until the path was clear and then ran as fast as I could back to the dinner tent.

One of the directors of Governor's Camp had raised a mongoose, and had given it the run of the camp, where it continued to hang around because of all the food and attention that it got. A striped, short-legged animal made famous by Rudyard Kipling in "Rikki-Tikki-Tavi," the mongoose is a member of the civet family and is known for its ability to kill snakes. Mongooses are not, as is often suggested, immune to the venom of poisonous snakes, but they are adept at dodging snakes' strikes, and by fluffing up their fur they cause snakes to misjudge striking distances. The mongoose at Governor's Camp would go from one tent to another, visiting. The guests would feed her eggs and talk to her, and she would respond with a funny cackling noise.

The shower at Governor's Camp was a cement slab with a curtain around it, out in the open. It was fancy for a tent camp, though—there was plumbing. One morning, I was busily cleaning up in the shower when something ran in, sank its teeth into my leg, and ran back out under the curtain. I was frightened momentarily, but I caught a glimpse of it and realized it was the mongoose, so I went on with my shower. She attacked me with her razor-sharp teeth three more times before I finished. I'd hear her cackling and know she was sneaking up on me, but I could never tell what angle she was coming from. By the time I finished washing, I had little bite marks all over my ankles. I found out afterward that the mongoose just didn't like people to take showers. All the people on my tour thought it was amusing that Joan Embery, animal handler, was attacked by a mongoose while showering in Africa.

From Governor's Camp, we headed south into Tanzania and Serengeti National Park, one of Africa's major wildlife preserves, spreading over 4,825 square miles. We drove slowly, viewing game throughout the day on our way to the Seronera Lodge, which is located in the heart of the Serengeti, close to major leopard and cheetah runs. The next day, we continued south, past the famous "kopjes," piles of boulders in which many types of game live.

We drove up into the mountains and spent the night at Wildlife Lodge, which has a spectacular view of Ngorongoro Crater, 12 miles across and 2,800 feet deep, formed by a volcanic eruption thousands of years ago. The following day we drove in Land-Rovers down a narrow, twisting dirt road into the crater and saw a tremendous abundance of wildlife—lions, rhinos, buffalos, elephants, and plains game—that lived in the bottom.

Our next stop was the Lake Manyara Hotel, high atop an escarpment with a beautiful view overlooking Lake Manyara in Lake Manyara National Park, which is known for its herd of over 200 elephants. One afternoon, after lazing in the swimming pool, I peered into the surrounding woods through the binoculars that were always ready on a stand by the pool and caught a glimpse of a pair of twin baby elephants. Twin elephants are exceedingly rare, and I had read about the pair at Manyara in a wildlife publication before I went to Africa.

After two more days of game drives in Tarangire National Park, we drove north to Arusha, the largest city in northern Tanzania, for a rest stop and shopping, then continued north and reentered Kenya. We traveled into the Amboseli Game Reserve and stayed at the Serena Amboseli Lodge, which is designed like a Masai village and faces Mt. Kilimanjaro, a gorgeous snow capped mountain that rises more than 19,000 feet.

From there we drove east to Tsavo West National Park, an 8,034-square-mile reserve known for its tremendous herds of "pink" elephants, which dust themselves with the reddish volcanic earth after they bathe. The volcanic scenery, with lava flows here and there, looked almost like a moonscape, and we saw leopards in the trees—the only leopards we spotted during the whole safari. We visited Kilaguni Lodge, where the dining area, the veranda, and private balconies on every room opened on three water holes. All through the day, while we dined and relaxed, elephants, zebras, rhinos, and buffalos came to drink and bathe, and colorful African birds, accustomed to human visitors, teased for food on the veranda.

The only thing that could be better than seeing Africa would be seeing Africa a second time, and I did that, two years after my first visit, when Keith Tucker put together another Safari with Joan Embery. The second trip took us to Kenya and Zambia.

This time we began our safari by driving north and northeast around Mount Kenya, to Meru National Park, where we saw Grévy's zebra, reticulated giraffes, blue-necked Somali ostriches, and many rare birds. It was here that the Adamsons of *Born Free* set their lioness, Elsa, free. We spent two nights at Meru Mulika Lodge, and among my souvenirs is a dung beetle I found dead on the lawn there. Dung beetles live in and feed on dung, and have flat, shovellike noses they use to roll it into piles.

On one of our game runs in Meru Park, we came across the Park's three southern white rhinoceroses—a bull, a cow, and her calf. The Park had only recently acquired five rhinos, but within a week, two had been killed by poachers. Two armed guards followed the remaining three all over the park, night and day, and they were so accustomed to having people around that we could pet them.

Among land mammals, rhinos are second in size only to elephants. Adults stand five or six feet high at the shoulder, are nine-and-a-half feet long, and weigh up to three tons. The distinctive upright horns on their snouts are not made of horn in the true sense, but are composed of closely packed horny fibers. Southern white rhinos are actually pale gray, and are more properly called square-lipped rhinos. The "white" in their name is derived from "wyd," which is Afrikaans for wide and refers to the animal's lip. Southern white rhinos have probably been saved from extinction by the efforts of Ian Player, the head of the Natal Parks Board in South Africa and the brother of golfer Gary Player. He developed a park where he bred the rhinos, and when their numbers had increased substantially, he began shipping them to zoos. The San Diego Wild Animal Park acquired twenty and had raised thirty-seven offspring as of this writing. But the three in Meru Park had to be guarded twenty-four hours a day.

Poachers slaughter rhinos only for their horns, which are ground up for use as an aphrodisiac that sells for about

$600 an ounce in the Orient. They leave the rest of the rhino's body to rot.

During my first trip to Africa, at Wilderness Trails, I saw a young bull elephant that had been killed a week before. The poachers had cut off its feet, which are made into ashtrays; its tail, the hair of which is made into bracelets; and its tusks, which are carved into decorative objects. The rest of the elephant lay shriveling in the sun. Unfortunately, preventing poaching in such huge game parks is almost impossible.

During my first safari, the stores in Kenya had been filled with items like zebra skin coasters and wall hangings, elephant-hide purses, elephant tusks, elephant-foot ashtrays, collabus monkey skins, wart hog tusks, and dik-dik horns. But before his death, President Kenyatta had banned the sale of all animal goods, and in 1978, the shops sold only sisal baskets, purses, mats, and ropes, wood-carvings, batik prints, and jewelry. Though welcome, Kenyatta's decision was essentially economic rather than humane; from a business point of view, it was more important to keep animals alive and propagating as tourist attractions than to sell their hides for immediate gain in gift shops.

From Meru we went to the Craigs' ranch for two days, then traveled up the slopes of Mt. Kenya to the Mountain Lodge, a treetop lodge facing a water hole and salt lick lit at night by floodlights. Each room had a balcony facing the water hole, and all one night I sat in the corner of mine, wrapped up in a blanket, watching elephants play.

Next we revisited the Masai Mara Game Reserve, where game is so plentiful, and stayed at the Mara Serena Lodge, a Masai-style lodge on a kopje overlooking the plains and

228

game. The lodge was known for its resident "mascot" elephant, a big male named Jumbo that would often walk right into camp, enticed by food left for him by visitors. He was a lone elephant; cows, calves and even adolescent elephants live in herds, but mature bulls are solitary except during mating.

At the camp entrance, there was a big sign saying, "Do not feed Jumbo. Do not encourage Jumbo," because he had become a menace. A visitor had once left food in his car, and Jumbo had broken into the car to get it. Since then, he would occasionally start pushing cars around, apparently looking for food. The situation had grown so bad that there was talk of killing Jumbo, since he was too big to crate and move elsewhere.

About one o'clock one morning, I heard a *crunch, crunch, crunch* outside my room. I got out of bed and tiptoed in the dark to my open window to look out. A few feet away stood Jumbo.

He was huge, easily ten feet tall. He looked right at me, and my heart started pounding. In that remote place, with no cars or planes disturbing the silence, I could hear Jumbo reach down with his trunk, grab a piece of grass, put it in his mouth, and grind it. I could hear him blow air out of his trunk. I stayed frozen by the window watching him eat until he finally meandered away. Despite all the time I'd spent with elephants, being that close to a wild bull was incredible.

Up early the next morning, I wandered around to the front of the lodge, right into a lot of commotion among a number of Africans in the parking lot. Jumbo, who even now could be seen standing by a water tank not far from the entrance to the lodge, had wandered into the parking lot and rolled two cars—he had literally picked them up and rolled them over, totally destroying them—and smashed the windows of two others. It was a funny feeling to see the destruction Jumbo had wrought only a short while after I, more fascinated than frightened, had watched him from my window.

From Mara Serena we headed back to Nairobi, and after a day to rest and pull ourselves together, we flew to Lusaka, Zambia, where we had to contend with a sticky political situation. We were met by a tour guide appointed by the government-run tourist bureau. When we were ready to leave the airport, some policemen started to drag away a nurse who was part of our tour group because she had taken pictures at the airport—she wanted a shot of a sign that said "Welcome to Zambia." Initially the police refused to let her go, but they finally settled for taking the film out of her camera, making her sign a lot of papers, and taking a police report on her.

Throughout Zambia, the police state atmosphere was very pronounced, and it was a very eerie feeling. We were prohibited from taking pictures of the House of Parliament or the police stations, and when we crossed the Kafue River, we saw a customs guard armed with a machine gun.

On our Zambian safari we traveled by bus to our camps. We started out in Kafue National Park, one of Africa's lushest and largest game parks, which covers 8,610 square miles. We did our game viewing in completely open Land-Rovers and on foot, accompanied by an armed guard as well as a nature guide.

To reach our first camp, Chunga Safari Village, we crossed the Kafue River on a quaint canopied wooden boat that made a perpetual *chung-chung-chung* noise and reminded all of us of the movie *The African Queen*. Later, while we were cruising the river on the same boat, we saw tremendous concentrations of bird life, as well as hippos and crocodiles.

230   The first night we were at Chunga camp, there were so many insects in the air that it's almost impossible to describe; the dinner table and all the lights were covered with them. They were in our glasses and on our food, and the little fly nets placed over everything were almost useless. Because it was a tsetse fly area, we had to take antimalaria pills, and after we left the camp, the bus was sprayed with insecticide. I'm one of those people whom insects really like to bite, and I was eaten up by tsetse flies, which look just like ordinary flies, but have a stinging bite.

We stayed two nights at Chunga camp, sleeping in simple reed and thatch huts overlooking the river. Our cots were surrounded by nets to keep off flies, mosquitoes, and other insects. When I awoke the first morning, I found dust in my hair and on my forehead and on my sleeping bag and cot. Termites had been eating at the thatched roof all night long. The second night I lay awake and heard them. It was incredible; it sounded like a hundred people eating.

Our third night in Kafue Park was spent in the Murungwa Safari Lodge, where there were still more insects—six-inch locusts that made American grasshoppers look like kids' stuff. I was fascinated by them but terrified at the same time—my old fear of bugs jumping on me was almost impossible to control.

My safaris left me with a new respect for the beauty of Africa's wild environment and real pain at the thought that there's little hope of it surviving in its present state. The safaris took us through the areas with the highest concentrations of game, but I was very aware that we seldom saw much game when we were traveling from one park to another. Farming was one major reason, and poaching another.

I wouldn't care if I never went anywhere else in my life, as long as I could continue to visit Africa. I enjoyed both my tour groups—it was fun to be able to share my experience of Africa with other people—and now I'd like to go back on my own and travel to specific places to see particular animals, free of the structure of a tour. During both my African trips, I felt very much at home; I liked the slow pace and found the people extremely interesting. I'd love to live in Africa, in an area where there are animals. Just knowing that they're around and seeing them pass occasionally would make me happy.

20

Horsin' Around

As my zoo career progressed, I continued to pursue my interest in horses, and at one point, to my delight, the two loves converged. In the fall of 1976, when Kathy and I were closing the show at Wegeforth Bowl, I was asked to go back to the Park and put together a horse show.

The range of entertainment available within the Park's village area had been steadily broadened. The animal show that Don McLennan ran had been divided; a new elephant trainer had been hired to do an elephant show while Don developed a horse show. But Don was leaving the Park, and since he had used several of his own horses in his show, I would be starting from scratch. I had total responsibility—I was to write a script, select music, budget the show, buy horses and equipment, hire personnel and

233

maintain work schedules for them, and train both the horses and people.

Though a horse show might seem out of place in a Park featuring exotic animals, the tremendous impact of humans on wild animal populations is no better illustrated than by a look at the domestic horse breeds that have been derived from wild stock. From wild ancestors, man has developed seventy different domestic breeds, selectively emphasizing particular traits for a variety of specific uses, from cattle herding to pleasure riding to racing. This theme gave relevance and continuity to the show.

I ended up showing ten different breeds, so I needed a considerable staff to pull it all together. Kathy moved with me to the Park to be one of the riders, and I inherited one rider from Don's show and hired another. There were also two guys who worked as stablehands and proppeople, and a couple of kids who helped out under a government-funded program.

We opened each performance by showing a Przewalski's horse, the wild ancestor of the domestic horse. This animal, the kind of horse ridden by Genghis Khan, is the last of the true wild horses. All other horses referred to as "wild" are actually "feral"—untamed animals derived from once-domesticated stock. The only wild equines in existence today—that includes asses, zebras, and Przewalski's horses—are confined to Asia and Africa.

Przewalski's horses once roamed the steppes of the Gobi Desert, but none was sighted between 1947 and 1965, and they were believed to be extinct in the wild. In 1966, six were seen in Mongolia, however, and others have been spotted since.

All Przewalski's horses now in captivity trace their ancestry to nine individuals, six wild specimens brought into

Europe about 1900, and three additional animals caught
later. Today there are over 300 Przewalski's horses in
major zoos around the world. The Halle-Prague Zoo keeps
the world pedigree book.

The first Przewalski's horses acquired by the San Diego
Zoo were two mares, Bonette and Belena, and a stallion,
Roland, all born at the Catskill Game Farm in New York
State in the early 1960's. Others were acquired in later
years, and several horses have been bred at the Zoo and
Wild Animal Park. Foals are named according to a system
that reflects their breeding; their names begin with the
first two letters of their mother's name. The names of all
horses descended from Bonnette begin with the letters *Bo*,
for example, and the names of those descended from
Belena begin with *Be*. The Przewalski's filly I used in the
horse show was called Bosaga.

Normally, the Przewalski's horses aren't handled, but
the night after Bosaga was born, her right hind leg was
broken—presumably another member of the herd stepped
on her. The Zoo chose to put her leg back together rather
than destroy her, and she was operated on the next day
at the Zoo hospital by Jane Meier and Phil Robinson.

Unlike human patients who can be told to stay in bed
or use crutches, most animals immediately try to use an
injured limb, and they often try to remove a heavy plaster
cast. "Bone plating"—screwing the broken ends of a bone
to a metal plate to bring them together, a technique used
in human medicine for many years—is being used with
increasing frequency in the Zoo hospital. In Bosaga's case,
a stainless steel plate and five screws were used to stabilize the fracture. The operation was successful, and
Bosaga, with her leg in a strong but light Fiberglas cast
that was replaced every seven to ten days, was raised in

the Care Center because of the frequent treatment she required. When she left there, she was given to the horse show.

Physically, Przewalski's horses bear a closer resemblance to asses and zebras than to domestic horses. They have shaggy coats ranging in color from light beige to golden tan, and like zebras and asses, they have a dorsal stripe— a dark stripe down the middle of the back—and a short, erect mane. Their tails, like those of zebras and asses, are made up of graduated lengths of hair, while domestic horses' tails are made up entirely of long hairs. They have no forelock, and they have blockier, less-refined heads than domestic horses. They're stocky animals. Horses range from fourteen hands to seventeen or eighteen hands at the shoulder, and Przewalski's horses are on the short end of that range.

They definitely have wild dispositions, and they develop strong preferences about the people that they will allow to approach them. Bosaga grew familiar with all of us who worked in the horse show, but when strangers approached her, she'd squeal and strike out at them with her feet. We had to warn visitors constantly. They'd walk along the row of horses, patting them all, and when they got to her stall, she'd try to nail them. Bosaga's wild temperament meant that any training would be limited, though Don Mc-Lennan had taught her to put her front feet up on a tub, and in time she grew so tame that we could sit on her back.

After we showed Bosaga, we brought on Eagle, my Thoroughbred, a horse bred for speed. Eagle did jumping, to show the horse's athletic ability, and performed some of the more impressive movements of dressage.

Then we showed Fairfax, my sister Janet's quarter horse,

a breed developed for use on ranches and for racing. Coming down the hill to the ring, Fairfax did a trail routine, working obstacles, going through gates and tires, and walking over a teeter-totter. Right on his heels came Alice, a burro, wearing a pack.

I got Alice through another trade with Dick Cessna, the man from whom I'd gotten Finally years before. Dick was living in a big development of ranch-style homes that had its own racetrack. In the middle of the racetrack was a huge lagoon, and Dick wanted two black swans for it. Casey Tibbs, a well-known rodeo star who also lived in the housing development, owned Alice. I arranged for Dick to get two swans from the Park and he arranged for the horse show to get the burro. Dick's the quintessential horse trader; he always finds a way to make a deal.

Next came Finally, my half Arabian. The oldest breed of horse, Arabians were developed for use in battle and for transportation. Finally performed a liberty routine. He was beautifully groomed and wore an elegant patent leather show harness and plumes, and I wore formal "appointments"—a black coat, top hat, stock tie, white britches, and black boots.

Next we showed Chips, a leopard Appaloosa, developed by American Indians for its color pattern. Chips was white with big black spots. He did a "gymkhana" routine—pole bending—maneuvering through a line of poles ten or fifteen feet apart, making a right around the first pole, a left around the next, a right around the next, and so on, like a slalom skier. Indians originally used these competitive games on horseback to train for battle, and today they're used for recreation.

We brought out a Clydesdale mare, Melodie, to show how large horses have been bred. Melodie was just under eighteen hands—six feet—at the shoulder. Such "draft" horses—Clydesdales are one of a number of big work breeds—were originally developed for use in battle in medieval times, when knights wore heavy armor. Later they were essential to the farming industry, until the development of modern machinery.

Bay-colored with white socks, Melodie was kind of lazy, but very good-tempered. Clydesdales have "feathers"— tufts of hair that go around their hooves and up the back of each leg—and every morning we bleached and scrubbed hers. Before every show, Melodie pulled a drag—a big piece of chain link fence with a telephone pole on it for weight—to smooth the soil in the ring.

With Melodie still in the ring, we'd bring on a miniature horse—a breed developed as novelty pets—to demonstrate that horses have also been bred *down* in size. When full grown, Atlas, our miniature, was about twenty-nine inches at the shoulder and weighed about 120 pounds. In winter he grew a very long, shaggy coat and looked like a little baby buffalo.

I got Atlas when he was just weaned, and I took him on "The Tonight Show" shortly after. We groomed him impeccably, and when I walked him onstage, everyone raved about how small he was. Johnny told me that as a child, he'd always wanted a pony for Christmas, and of course I told him that the same was true of me. When it was time to leave, Atlas didn't want to walk through the curtain, so I picked him up and carried him off. "That's really the kind of horse a cowboy ought to have," Johnny remarked. "If the horse gives him a hard time, he can just pick him up and carry him."

We'd been struck by a long period of cold weather and heavy rains and floods—unusual for San Diego—so after the show, I kept Atlas in my house. He lived there for about a month, until the rain stopped. He got along with all three of my dogs, and had a little dish right next to theirs. In fact, he lived much like a dog. He slept in the living room on the carpet, and he had free run of the house. He was pretty well housebroken; I'd put him outside and he'd go and then I'd bring him back in.

Atlas was very affectionate and liked to sit in my lap or lean against me or lay his head on my lap. He went everywhere—sort of the horse show mascot—riding in the cab of my pickup, standing on the floor on the right side with his head on the seat. Atlas loved attention, and he really thought he should be around people. He'd go walking through the offices at the Park, and between horse shows, he'd come and stand in the tack room while we ate lunch.

Horses have been selectively bred not only for speed, color, and size, but for gait. Tennessee walkers, bred for a special four-beat "running walk" that remains very comfortable even when performed at speed, were ridden by Southern plantations owners when they inspected their crops. They can go as fast at the walk as most horses can go at a fast trot, and can go a long time without tiring. Their gait is so smooth that you could carry a glass of water while riding one and not spill a drop.

The ability to walk comes through breeding, but training is required to bring it out, and there are a lot of walking horses around that have never really been taught to walk. Show-quality walkers are very expensive, but I managed to find a retired show horse, Mighty Miss, a big chestnut mare about fifteen years old. Mighty Miss was an old pro. She knew her job and would walk the ring with almost no guidance.

In the 1800's and early 1900's women rode sidesaddle, because they wore long skirts and because it was considered improper to ride astride like a man. We demonstrated sidesaddle riding on Wally, another Arab. Our beautiful sidesaddle outfit—a long flowing skirt, a jacket with lace cuffs and choker, and a top hat—added an elegant touch to the horse show, since for all the other events we wore britches or jeans.

To end the show, a matched pair of ponies, Coco and Sir Lancelot, or Lance, pulled a cart with a fringed top to the strains of "Surrey with the Fringe on Top."

You would have to spend two days at a regular horse show to sample all the events we showed. I rode, at various times, in all the events, though my favorites were dressage, jumping, and sidesaddle.

Actually, performing in the ring was a small part of the work involved in putting on the show. We spent the first three hours of every single morning washing and grooming the horses, because we showed each one "turned out" at it would be in a formal horse show. We also had to scrub and oil all the tack, rake the ring, and set the jumps.

A lot of people say horses are stupid, and it's true that they're not extremely intelligent. But I've always felt that the challenge of working with them lies in being able to put your brain and their physical capabilities together. Horse and rider must be a team.

It can take a horse days or weeks to learn what an elephant can learn in twenty minutes or half an hour, and it takes a tremendous amount of repetition to train one. Because horses have a very short attention span and are easily distracted and easily spooked, training them is similar in many ways to training wild animals. In general, as long as they're familiar with their surroundings, they work well, but when they become frightened, they can be dangerous. They can injure people and they can injure themselves, because when they're in trouble they may panic. I've seen frightened horses run through fences and come out the sides of horse trailers. You really have to use caution when you work around them. They're very strong, and you can't overpower them physically, just as you can't overpower an elephant. You have to work on them mentally, make it easier for them to do the right thing than the wrong thing.

Early in 1978, Bosaga reached breeding age, and the curators told me they had promised her to the Denver Zoo as a breeding loan. The shipment of Bosaga and two other Przewalskis had already been arranged, but I said that if I could keep Bosaga in the show through the summer, I would haul her to Denver myself in the fall.

I took her to Denver in November. The trip coincided with my appearance on a segment of "Switch," the detective series starring Eddie Arnold and Robert Wagner. The story was set in the Zoo, and I was to play myself. I had already made plans to haul Bosaga when they wrote me into the script, so I had to make the trip in four days flat, in order to get back in time to start shooting. A friend rode with me, and we drove almost around the clock, just stopping along the highway now and then to sleep for a few hours. When we stopped in New Mexico to get gas and check on Bosaga, a man said, "My, that's a handsome-looking mule you have there." We just smiled and said, "Thank you."

We reached Denver at night. The people at the zoo there asked a couple of questions about Bosaga and some publicity pictures were taken. They had a cement barn with a big stall all fixed up for her with a heat lamp and water and fresh bedding. She was a little nervous, almost like a little kid who's awakened in the middle of the night and doesn't know where she is or what's going on. All of us in the show had grown very attached to her and it was hard to hand her over, but I had known for a long time that it was coming, so I was prepared.

I loved running the horse show more than anything I'd ever done before. I would have been willing to do it for the next twenty years. I've always loved being in a stable, even if I'm only mucking stalls. Working animals like Carol and Cody involves a considerable mental challenge, but riding horses is also a physical challenge, requiring balance and timing and the coordinated and sensitive use of hands and legs.

I put a lot of effort into the show, and when I got it put together I was really proud of it. But after two years, in September 1978, it was discontinued for budgetary reasons.

A long period of rain and floods early in 1978 contributed to the decision. When it rains, you can work birds and even elephants, but not horses, and more important, the overall revenue lost by the Zoo and Park during the weeks of rain helped create pressure to cut costs.

The horse show did have a greater overhead than any of the other shows. We used to spend two hundred dollars every six weeks just to keep the horses in shoes, and we had a big investment in riding outfits and tack.

The show closed on Labor Day. At the conclusion of the final performance, those of us who were riding lined up on our horses in the ring. I was on Eagle. The announcer started to say that this was the last show and that he wanted to thank everyone who had worked on it, and I rode out of the ring right in the middle of it because I was in tears and I didn't think I was going to be able to stand in line.

It was probably the worst night I've ever had. The rest of the girls and their boyfriends all went out for a kind of bittersweet celebration, but I stayed late and packed up all the equipment that I had brought to the Park for the show and went home. When I left, it was like walking away from everything I'd worked for.

21

*Changing
Times*

I spent the next week selling horses and tack and cleaning up the facilities. It was extremely painful to have to sell all the horses I had picked myself and grown so fond of. I ended up buying Alice the burro and one of the ponies, and I kept the Clydesdale at my place for a while, too, until the decision was made to put her in the Children's Zoo. I was feeling low and empty, so I took time off to get ready for my second trip to Africa, figuring I'd start all over again when I got back.

When I did, I spent the first few months updating my files and getting caught up on everything, because for two years I had been so wrapped up in the horse show that I'd been out of touch with all the other things that were going on around the Zoo and the Park. I was depressed the whole time. I missed being outdoors working with animals, and I missed the demands that a daily show placed on my intelligence and creativity. The whole reason I had gone to work at the Zoo was to work with animals, and suddenly I wasn't doing it anymore. Because of the enormous audience reached by television, the Zoo was still willing to have me take animals to shows, but they had become more conservative about letting me take animals out before the general public for speeches and appearances. For the first time, I began to make appearances alone, without animals.

Several factors had contributed to the Zoo management's altered attitude. One was the volume of restrictive legislation concerning the handling of exotic animals that had been enacted in the years since I'd first started working in the public-relations department. Legislation affecting zoos has increased tenfold in the past twelve years, so much that those who operate zoos are becoming worried about their continued freedom to manage animals.

Of course, the burgeoning volume of laws is the result of increased public interest in halting the destruction of exotic species, and one of the main reasons I make appearances is to make people aware of what's happening to animals in the wild. But the beneficial result of such education—protective legislation—actually restricts how I do my job. Today, the trip I made through Colorado and Arizona with Robella would be so complicated by laws controlling the shipment of endangered animals that the Zoo might not contemplate it.

Zoos have to conform to the regulations of many agencies, among them the federal Department of Agriculture, which sets quarantines and conducts health inspections of animals and plants in order to prevent the communication of diseases to agricultural animals; the Department of

Health, Education and Welfare, which conducts primate health inspections to prevent the communication of diseases from animals to humans; the Department of the Interior, which regulates shipments of endangered species across state lines; the Department of Commerce, which is responsible for marine mammals' protection; the Customs Department, which regulates the importation of animals; and state fish and game departments, which protect native animals.

The Animal Welfare Act, passed in 1970, establishes standards for humane handling, care, and transportation of all warm-blooded animals and empowers the USDA to license and inspect zoos. Other laws, like the Marine Mammal Protection Act of 1972 and the Endangered Species Act of 1973, are primarily intended to prevent the commercial slaughter of rare animals, but do require zoos to acquire extensive permits to obtain certain species.

I and other members of the zoological profession agree in principle with most laws concerning the conservation of wild animals and their humane treatment in captivity— indeed, individual professionals have furnished much of the information important in the formulation of these laws. Regulations controlling zoos have a positive value and have definitely led to improved conditions for animals.

Currently there are efforts underway on the part of zoo groups to establish accreditation for zoos, which would then exempt them from some government regulations. Indeed, the Zoological Action Committee, Inc. (ZOOACT), a nonprofit corporation, was organized in September 1974 to lobby in Washington, D.C., and state capitals on behalf of responsible zoos and relieve them from some of the burdens of legislation that is really directed against badly managed zoos, road shows, private owners who do not know how to maintain exotics properly, and people who exploit animals for commercial reasons.

Tough legislation does cut down the number of people exploiting animals out of self-interest. People who are willing to work within legal guidelines are people whose main interest is their animals.

The number of appearances I made with animals also decreased because the Zoo management had become more liability conscious.

Not without reason. Several years ago, a young Zoo visitor scaled the wall surrounding "Wolf Woods" and was attacked by the wolves and sustained puncture wounds before he was rescued. His father, a lawyer, immediately sued the Zoo, even though the boy had willfully climbed into the enclosure. Though it was believed that the Zoo had an easily defensible position, the case was settled out of court, with the Zoo paying the boy's medical expenses.

Not long after, another Zoo visitor crawled off the moving sidewalk, hung his arm over the fence, and had his hand bitten by the wolves. Then, in 1973, a twelve-year-old Mexican boy visiting the Zoo tried to go through the enclosure to take a shortcut. In this case, the boy couldn't read the signs identifying the animals, but he did jump over the moving sidewalk that runs past the wolf enclosure and scale the wall, which is eight to ten feet high at that point. When he saw the wolves, he became frightened and turned around to run back, but he fell, and a group of wolves attacked him, inflicting puncture wounds and lacerations on his chest, arms, and feet. A security guard had to kill one wolf and wound another in order to rescue him. Once again, the Zoo was sued.

Foolhardiness and vandalism on the part of a few visitors are perpetual problems for zoos. Today several of the beautiful moated enclosures at the Zoo are surrounded by high fences that have nothing to do with containing animals. They've been put up because people throw junk that might frighten or injure animals—lighted cigarettes, glass, horrible things—into the enclosures. The problem has grown especially serious since certain species have become so scarce and so costly. We have such a fence around our moated pygmy chimpanzee enclosure, because we just can't risk having such a rare animal hurt.

After the third wolf incident, the Zoo moved the wolves from Wolf Woods, a half-acre enclosure constructed at great cost to show the animals in a large wooded area, as you would find them in nature, and returned them to a more confined area. The incidents really brought home to the Zoo management the Zoo's increasing legal vulnerability—they realized that juries were becoming more likely to award damages to people who were hurt as a consequence of their own recklessness.

Quite early in my career, I took Toby, a tiger that had been raised in the nursery and Children's Zoo, to a Cub Scout dinner. Toby was several months old and had reached a pretty good size. There was a large group of boys at the dinner, and Red and I told them that they had to approach Toby one at a time, moving quietly and petting him without doing anything to frighten him. But a couple of kids didn't listen and came running up, and Toby bit one of them. It's a perpetual problem—even if I have control of an animal, I can never completely control the actions of people around me.

The boy wasn't badly hurt, but a lawyer immediately called the boy's parents and offered to represent them for a percentage of the amount they might ultimately receive in court. The parents, fans of the Zoo, didn't pursue any legal action. But in recent years, many people have grown "sue-happy," and the Zoo management has become very reluctant to let me take cats or other animals that can bite or scratch people out around the public.

By the time the horse show ended, all the animals that I'd maintained for my use had been transferred or shipped out and sold, because I wasn't handling them regularly. During the last months of the show, Kathy had been called back to the Zoo to run a new show in Wegeforth Bowl on her own, and Rufus was in that. She didn't use Cody, who had always frightened her somewhat and who had grown bad-tempered because of arthritis as he got older, so he had been given away and was scheduled to be shipped out. Carol had remained at the Zoo for a while after I began doing the horse show, but once it became apparent that I'd be so involved with the horses, she had been sent to the Park to be part of the elephant show, in which she continued to perform many of the things that I had trained her to do, including painting. That was the hardest thing for me to take.

Most of the animals that were available to me for television appearances were under the control of the education department or the Children's Zoo. For the first time in years, I wasn't directly responsible for any Zoo animals, and sometimes I felt that there was no reason to go to work in the morning.

I was also going through a more personal, though related, crisis. For ten years, I had put all my energies into succeeding in my profession and making something of my job. But my devotion to my work had taken its toll on my personal relationships.

I'd always felt that to do it right, I had to give my job top priority in my life. I couldn't see a way to compromise that. But it's hard to give your job that kind of energy and attention and still have a life of your own. I had always been so happy in my work that I never thought I could want anything more. But at last I began to ask, "Isn't there more to life than this?"

22
Coming Home

I've been told that in Chinese the word for "crisis" is the same as the word for "opportunity." After months of depression, I knew I had to figure out how I could take what I had and do something more with it. I didn't want to underestimate the value of my ambassadorial role just because I liked to work animals. I think what I do is important.

After considerable thought, I decided to go back to school, enrolling in telecommunications at San Diego State. I've never aspired to a career in television—I think of my talk-show appearances as a small part of what I do—but since I found myself being pushed into the field more and more, I decided that I wanted to function as professionally as possible. I began by choosing courses from which I thought I could gain immediate value. I

253

wanted to learn to deal more effectively with the people who are necessary to create a film or television show. I wanted to learn industry terminology, to be able to talk with people at television stations and understand what they're looking for. I wanted to learn to handle a show without relying on conversation with a host.

So I began learning, in school, about what I'd been doing for the previous ten years. Being back in college was a very pressured situation, because I wanted to prove myself—to myself, and to the department. The Telecommunications Department at SDSU is essentially closed—the only way to get in is to petition—and it was very important to me to show the school that I was capable of doing the work even though I had a full-time job. I also wanted to do well because the Zoo allowed me to arrange my work schedule around school, even though I continued putting in a full forty-hour week.

But I love school. Going back has given me new things to think about and a chance to develop more in an area that I find very challenging and creative.

Even while I was relieving some of my frustration by resuming my education, I talked again and again with the Zoo management about my desire to work with animals, and finally they told me to start training Devi, the Children's Zoo's present elephant, and Sandy, a young dromedary. Sometimes working with Devi makes me feel like I'm starting all over again, but I once again look forward to going to work in the morning, because I know I'll be greeted when I get there by one of my favorite creatures, a baby elephant.

In 1977, when I was still running the horse show, one of the original riders left, and I hired Torrey Pillsbury, a petite and pretty eighteen-year-old stock-horse riding champion, to take her place. One night, she brought her father, Duane, to see the show.

I was watering and feeding all the horses when she introduced us. Duane was slender and distinguished-looking, with blue eyes, silver hair, and the rugged tan of an outdoorsman. He was dressed in jeans, boots, and a cowboy hat. He pitched right in to help me, and I liked him immediately. He was soft-spoken and had a ready smile, and he struck me as a truly nice person, easy to get along with. Duane was the real estate coordinator for the Grossmont Community College system in San Diego and a real estate broker, but his hobby was horses. When we got through tending the horses, we went out to dinner, discovered our mutual interest, and made a date for me to haul Finally to Duane's ranch and go riding with him.

After that, we became great friends. We took our horses to the mountains and the deserts to ride. I looked on it as an ideal situation, because there was no chance of our getting involved—Duane was nearly twenty years older than I. I had a good friend to spend time with, but wasn't tied down to what I had come to think of as the demands of a relationship.

Duane's marriage of eighteen years had ended two years before, and just before we met, his house had burned to the ground in a terrible fire from which he and his two daughters had been lucky to escape with their lives. They had lost everything inside. I admired Duane, because he was raising two teen-agers and trying to put his life back together and somehow, in the midst of such tragedy and stress, he enjoyed life more than any person I knew.

Gradually, our friendship grew into love, and age was no barrier. We just spent more and more time together, and we were having such a good time that we never stopped to think about it.

I felt very relaxed around Duane. I never felt I had to choose between him and my job and my other interests. He was happy to spend time with me whenever I had time to spend, and he liked to do the things I liked to do—his own animals included five quarter horses and a Great Dane. Duane was secure enough to delight in my success and be tolerant of the demands of my career. He was truly interested in what I did, and he got a kick out of my professional adventures.

Duane had lived on his ranch for four years before his house burned. The ranch had been a lifelong dream for him. Like me, he grew up wanting to live where he could keep horses, and he had worked very hard to get there.

When we met, the ruins of his house had been leveled, and there was nothing on his property but an old barn and his horses. When he began building his new house, I was involved in every step, because I wanted to help him and because I wanted to learn all about building houses. Night after night we worked together on his new home, roofing it, painting it, staining it, and discussing every purchase for it.

It's a wood ranch-style house with a shake-shingle roof and a porch the full length of the front. It has beamed ceilings, oak floors, and lots of windows. And it sits on sixteen acres in Lakeside, in the heart of San Diego horse country, surrounded by beautiful mountains.

When Duane first visited my house in Lemon Grove, he was very taken with the old stirrups, glass jars, and wooden decoys that I'd collected and decorated with. So when we began to work on his house, we began collecting antiques that would look good inside. It became another shared interest. For the mantel on the huge living room fireplace, I picked up an old pylon from the Coronado Ferry at a friend's ranch and hauled it to Duane's house in my truck, almost wiping out a traffic signal on the way because the pylon was so long. For the yard, we found a hitching post and some antique wagons.

After a while, Duane began to say that I had put so much work into the house that I ought to be around to enjoy it when it was finished. I was already spending so much time there that keeping up my own rented place in Lemon Grove—a big house with a huge lawn and corrals and boarded horses I had to care for—was becoming impossible. It seemed more logical to move my horses to Duane's ranch and take an apartment close by.

On August 5, 1979, we were married in an outdoor ceremony at the ranch. I wore an old-fashioned muslin dress with a matching hat, and Duane and I drove up in an antique carriage pulled by Finally. Afterward, we had a big barbecue with a country and western band.

In a way, crazy as it sounds, the only thing that wasn't perfect was the ranch. I'm not sure why, but I've always had a drive to fulfill my goals on my own. From the time I wanted a horse as a kid and decided I was going to work until I had one, I've set out to get the things I wanted, one by one. My ultimate goal was to buy a house and property.

When Duane and I first talked about marriage, I said, "There's only one problem. I've worked so hard to be able to get a house and land on my own that in some way I don't want you to spoil it by giving it to me." It meant so much to me that Duane and I even discussed the possibility of my going ahead and buying a house and renting it out. But it would be kind of silly for both of us to have a home and property, which take a lot of time to keep up. And sharing the love and care that went into building the new house has made our ranch truly ours.

Anyway, a ranch is something to build, to work on. I've spent years working on other people's places, only to have them raise the rent out of reach or decide they want to use it themselves so that I have to move and see all my work come to nothing. Keeping horses has made my life a battle from one payday to another, and it's been a continual struggle to live where I could have animals. It's nice to have a place at last that no one can take away, where no one can say that I can't tie a horse here or build a pen there.

For the first time in ten years, my life has another dimension than the Zoo. For a long time, I never thought I'd feel the need of anything else, but now I see that it's important for my life to have some balance. Duane's daughters, Torrey and Holly, are still at home with us, so after years as a single person, I have a family again.

Duane and I are happy spending time together, even when we're working. One of my favorite times comes when we go out in the evening to feed and check all the animals and fuss over the plants we're raising. We stretch it out, letting the dogs and the pig out to run and lingering to pat and talk to all the horses till the sun drops behind the mountain.

23

The Star on the
Dressing-Room Door

Even during my unhappiness after the closing of the horse
show, I always knew how lucky I was to have my job. Just
by virtue of its size and numerous departments, a zoo the
size of ours has internal disputes over money and priorities;
everybody has a different idea of how they'd like to see
things done. But the San Diego Zoo is still one of the best
in the world at what it does, and it still represents the only
alternative to the destruction of many animals in the wild.

When I went to work at the Zoo, I never dreamed I'd
be able to become so intimately involved with exotic animals. My job has enabled me to develop a variety of skills,
including animal training, public speaking, and dealing
with people. I've had the opportunity to travel and meet
fascinating people.

Materially, though my job hasn't made me rich, it has

allowed me to have more tangible things. I always wanted horses, and today I have them. Then I longed for a truck and horse trailer, and now I have them. Then I wanted to have my own furniture, because when I moved out of my parents' home I didn't have anything, and piece by piece, I was able to fill an entire house with furniture. I have snow skis and water skis and scuba diving equipment so that I can enjoy the sports I love.

I've put together the kind of life I always thought I wanted. It hasn't been easy. I've had to pick and choose and budget and wait. I've had to struggle to make things work the way I want in my life. I didn't go out and party a lot or go hog-wild on clothes, but of course, I've always been more inclined to spend $60 on a pair of riding britches than to buy something to wear to work.

When I give a lecture, the person who introduces me usually goes through a list of my achievements in the past decade, saying that I've trained animals, managed exotic animal and horse shows, appeared on numerous national talk shows, and traveled all over this country and to Europe and Africa. After this big buildup, I always feel that I have to live up to impossible expectations in my audience's minds. So to break the ice, I often tell them that I really enjoy my job, and that, admittedly, when I started doing national television shows, I thought it was pretty impressive. Then I recall my appearance on "The Steve Allen Show" with Carol in January of 1971. Whenever people say to me, "Isn't it great that you do all these TV shows, that you get all this fame?" I always think of that experience.

It was only the second national show I'd ever been on, and on my way up to the studio in Los Angeles, I thought about how I'd always heard that each guest on such shows has a star on his dressing-room door. When I arrived, I had a lot of things that had to be moved to my dressing room, so I headed down the hall looking for it, and sure enough, every door had a star with a name on it. At the end of the row, there was a great big, really nice dressing room, and the star on the door said, "Carol the Elephant."

I had to laugh. At the time, I had no public identity whatsoever—I didn't even know I was going to have my job for more than a year. Since then, I've become better known, and there's been a little more media interest in me as a person, but I wouldn't be on television if it weren't for the animals. My job is to pull everything together and represent this group of exotic animals that can't speak for themselves. For years, when I was asked if I wanted to stay on shows to talk after displaying animals, I'd say no, because I never felt it was my role to speak as an individual. Through the years I've worked for the Zoo and through all the experiences the job has given me, I've never forgotten the lesson I learned that night in the hallway at the "The Steve Allen Show." The Zoo's animals—rare, beautiful and fascinating creatures—have always been the stars.

Books on Animals

These books answer many of the general questions that animal lovers often ask.

Bird Families of the World. Harrison, C.J.O., ed. New York: Abrams, 1978.

Bresland, Osmond P. *Animal Life and Lore.* Revised ed. New York: Harper & Row, 1972. (A catalog of animal facts)

Campbell, Sheldon. *Lifeboats to Ararat.* New York: Times Books, 1978. (Insights into the inner workings of zoos and their modern role as preserves for endangered species)

Conant, Roger. *A Field Guide to Reptiles and Amphibians of Eastern and Central North America.* 2nd ed. Boston: Houghton Mifflin Co., 1975.

Crandall, Lee S. *The Management of Wild Mammals in Captivity.* Chicago: Univ. of Chicago Press, 1964. (This book and Walker's *Mammals of the World,* below, are the "bibles" of zoo people, and are helpful for those seeking background on exotic animals and guidelines for their care.)

Curtis, Lawrence. *Zoological Park Fundamentals.* Wheeling, WV: American Association of Zoological Parks and Aquariums. (How to start a zoo)

Douglas-Hamilton, Iain and Oria. *Among the Elephants.* New York: Viking Press, 1975. (One of the few books on the behavior of elephants in the wild.)

Fowler, Murray E. *Restraint and Handling of Wild and Domestic Animals.* Ames, IA: Iowa State Univ. Press, 1978.

Gzimek, Bernard. *Animal Life Encyclopedia . . . including Ecology, Ethology and Evolution.* New York: Van Nostrand Reinhold Co., 1974, 75, 77. (A multivolume guide to animals from invertebrates to higher mammals, written by a German zoo director. It's got everything.)

Hediger, Heini. *The Psychology and Behavior of Animals in Zoos and Circuses.* New York: Dover Publications, 1968.

Hill, Clyde A., William C. Warren, and Edward E. Wolfe. *AAZPA Manual of Federal Wildlife Regulations.* Wheeling, WV: American Association of Zoological Parks and Aquariums, 1979.

Hodge, Guy R. *Careers: Working with Animals.* The Humane Society of the United States, 2100 L Street, N.W., Washington, D.C. 20037. (Includes information on education, career guidance publications and periodicals that list available positions. Available by mail from the Society.)

The Merck Veterinary Manual. 4th ed. Siegmund, O.H., ed. Rahway, NJ: Merck & Co., 1973.

Minton, Sherman, and M. Minton. *Giant Reptiles.* New York: Charles Scribners Sons, 1973.

Schmidt & Inger. *Living Reptiles of the World.* Garden City, NY: Hanover House, 1957.

Stebbins, Robert C. *A Field Guide to Western Reptiles and Amphibians.* Boston: Houghton-Mifflin Co., 1966.

Walker, Ernest P. *Mammals of the World.* 3rd ed. Baltimore and London: Johns Hopkins Univ. Press, 1975. (Two volumes)

Williams, John G. *A Field Guide to the National Parks of East Africa.* London: Collins, 1967.

Zoo & Aquarium Careers. American Association of Zoological Parks and Aquariums, Oglebay Park, Wheeling, WV, 26003. (A pamphlet on career opportunities, available by mail from the Association.)

Zoo and Wild Animal Medicine. Fowler, Murray E., ed. Philadelphia, London and Toronto: W.B. Saunders Co., 1978.